PSYCHEDELIC SEX VAMPIRES

Glitter
books

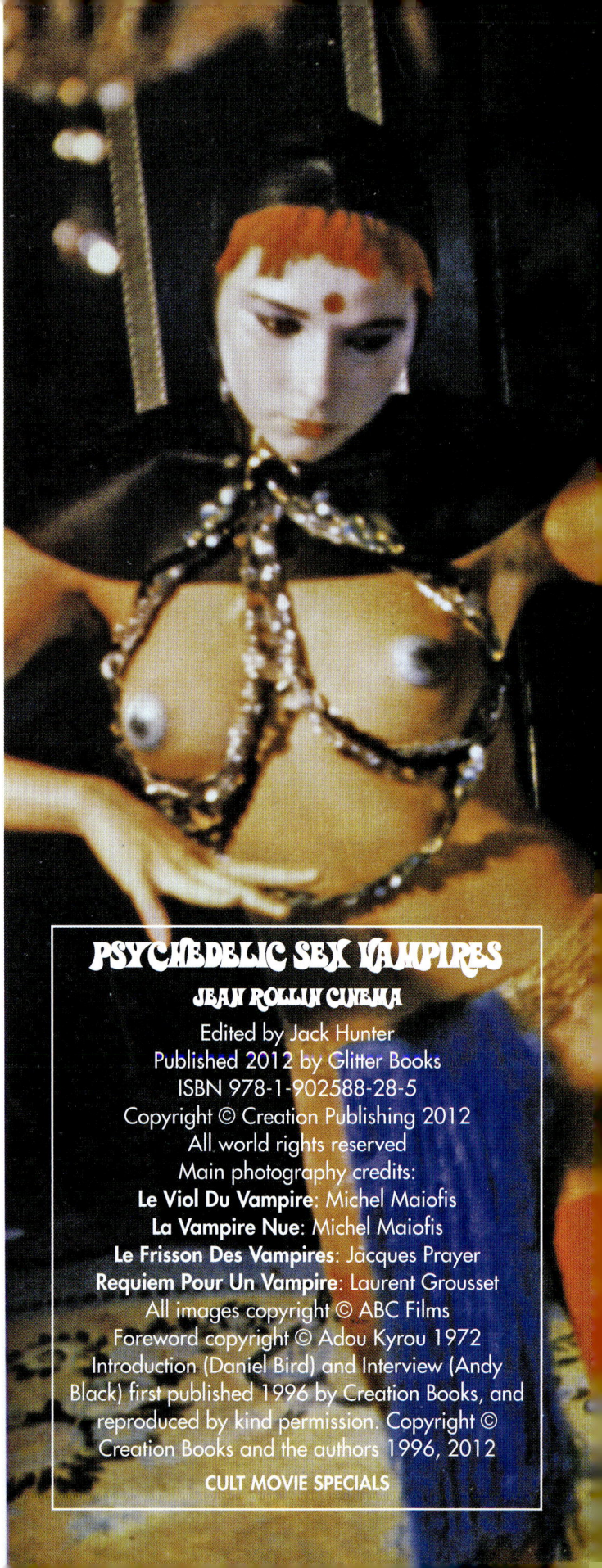

PSYCHEDELIC SEX VAMPIRES

JEAN ROLLIN CINEMA

Edited by Jack Hunter
Published 2012 by Glitter Books
ISBN 978-1-902588-28-5
Copyright © Creation Publishing 2012
All world rights reserved
Main photography credits:
Le Viol Du Vampire: Michel Maiofis
La Vampire Nue: Michel Maiofis
Le Frisson Des Vampires: Jacques Prayer
Requiem Pour Un Vampire: Laurent Grousset
All images copyright © ABC Films
Foreword copyright © Adou Kyrou 1972
Introduction (Daniel Bird) and Interview (Andy
Black) first published 1996 by Creation Books, and
reproduced by kind permission. Copyright ©
Creation Books and the authors 1996, 2012

CULT MOVIE SPECIALS

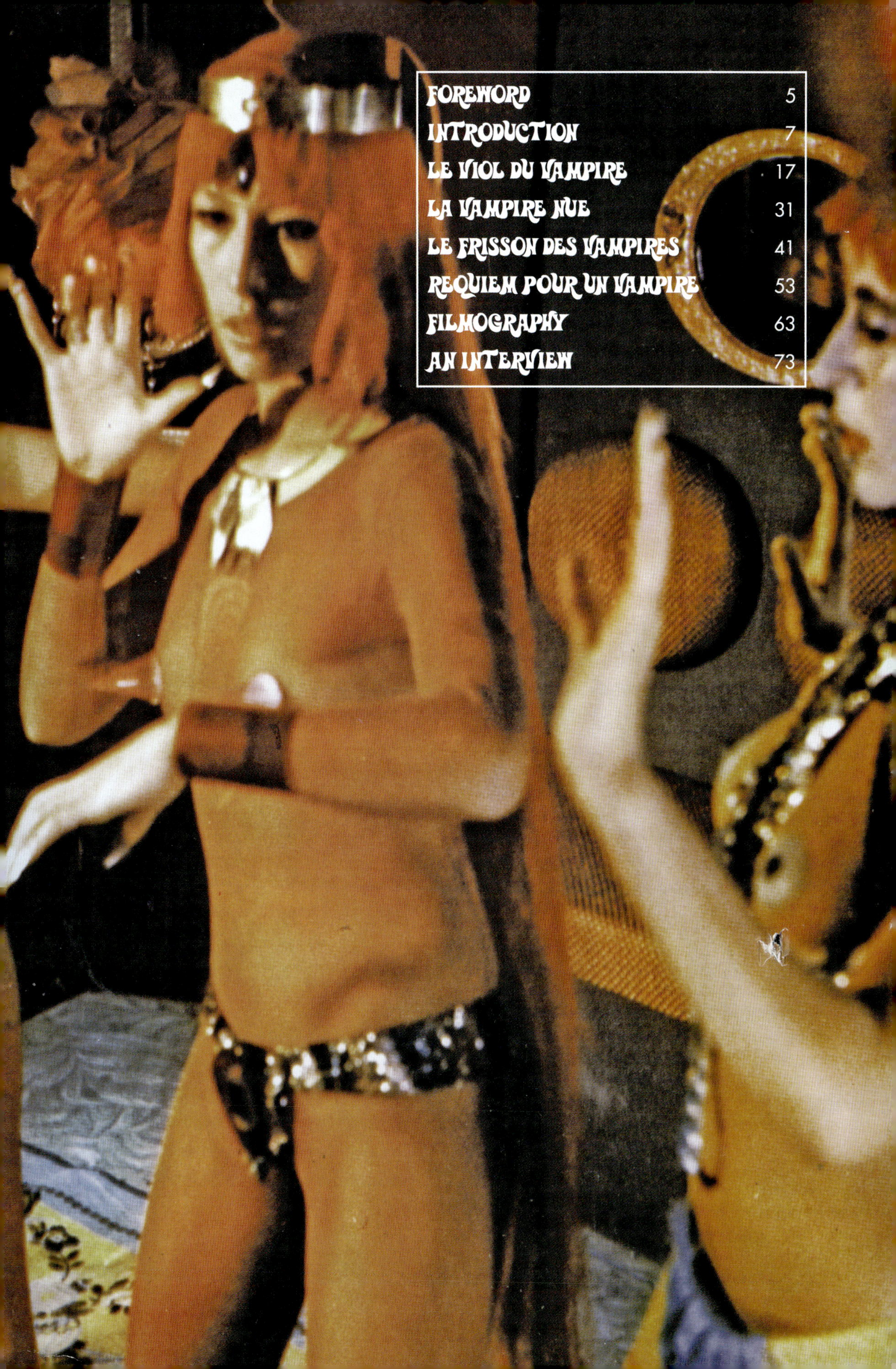

THE VAMPIRES OF JEAN ROLLIN HAVE NO FEAR OF THE CRUCIFIX

All the photographs in this book are from the films of Jean Rollin. They do not reveal those films, but reflect them in the mirror of chance. They express the freedom of cinema itself.

Like several of his masters (Josef von Sternberg, for example), Rollin uses his scenarios to unleash games of ecstasy and danger. Most notably, he uses collage, ordaining his encounters with a rigorous *naïveté*. At this level the notion of quality becomes irrelevant. Can one speak of the 'quality" of the paintings of Clovis Trouille?

Two girls dressed as clowns shudder with fear in a palpably haunted château, a sedan-chair finds new uses, and a vampire bat becomes a *câche-sexe*.

Le Viol Du Vampire is a quasi-automatic film with no defined subject. It has a vampire marriage, a psycho-analyst who does not believe in vampires yet becomes a vampire, a vampire priest, etc. Its black humour is reflexive.

In **La Vampire Nue**, the guests at a bizarre ceremony agree to kill themselves so that their blood can nourish the film's heroine. Two groups of vampires engage in a game of death.

In **Le Frisson Des Vampires**, two undead brothers live in a château with their common mistress. The master of the world sends amongst them a strange female vampire, whose task is the save the vampire race.

In **Requiem For A Vampire**, the vampires are exhausted. They have neither the power nor the desire to spread their disease. Is this the end?

In all these films, eroticism plays the same role as black humour: it demystifies, shuffles the cards, lays false tracks, terminating in a cry of ecstasy or screams of terror.

And yet Rollin is serious. He has met a *real* vampire, and one of these days he will make a film written by that vampire.

The time is approaching when vampires will seize their own destiny, fashion their own cinema. Rollin will help them beyond bounds.

Why should the vampire be considered as evil? It is obvious that sucking, biting, and transformation are all characteristics of the vampire, making him a symbol of sexuality; for that reaason he is considered malevolent.

He is sin. Therefore, he fears the cross.

Luckily, Richard Matheson in his estimable *I Am Legend* has destroyed all the idealistic Christian arguments, returning the vampire to his rightful status: that of a "normal" being.

In 1949, the killer John Haigh wrote in his prison cell, while waiting for his execution: "...I

made an incision in her throat and drank a glass of her blood. She was wearing a crucifix around her neck. I experienced an infinite joy in desecrating it."

Now the churches are deserted, and ex-believers haunt cinemas, watching horror films. The notion of God no longer inspires fear, the Pope is just a well-paid executive, and it follows that in the near future he will be ruined, blown up with dynamite, allowing the insurgency of a free cinema.

We are allowed to dream, after all.

This book is also a dream.

—Ado Kyrou

FASCINATION

Since 1968 English-speaking cinephiles have tended to resist Jean Rollin's work, his descents into hermetically sealed worlds of desolate châteaus, solitary vampires and violent seduction, and above all the bizarre genius and poetic imagery with which he weaves his morbid fascinations. Unlike many filmmakers, Rollin's lineage is one of writers, poets, painters, serialists, and comic strip artists as well as cinéastes. The vampire, the (pair of) virgin(s), and the castle form the cardinal points of Rollin's art.

The vampire is often portrayed as the embodiment of both sex and death, so it seems natural that Rollin's perception lies confined to more salacious variations of the "exploitation filmmaker" legend. However, despite these "low art" connotations, his nocturnal fantasies perhaps dwell more readily in the company of those belonging to Tristan Corbière, Gaston Leroux and Jean Ray rather than those of, say, Jess Franco. Although Leroux's *Phantom Of The Opera* is widely acknowledged as one of the great horror novels, not only does it remain little read, but it eclipses the rest of his body of work. Although Leroux's detective novels *The Perfume Of The Woman In Black* and *The Mystery Of The Yellow Room* have both been filmed, his extraordinary, and rather horrific, short Grand-Guignol tales remain trapped in obscurity. These are lurid pulp pieces which have undoubtedly made a huge impression on Rollin. Several of these stories, notably *The Woman With The Velvet Collar*, are prefaced with a maritime scenario of sailors reciting weird tales at coastal taverns, which is perhaps why this location has such resonance in Rollin's films, particularly **Les Démoniaques**. The element of organised crime present in Leroux's novels also proliferates into almost every Rollin opus, from bandits in **Le Viol Du Vampire**, **Fascination** and **Les Démoniaques** to the runaways in **Requiem Pour Un Vampire**, **Nuit Des Traquées** and **The Escapees**.[1]

Tristan Corbière's poetry has a romantic preoccupation with memories. Perhaps it is this one vein which runs consistently through Rollin's films, lending them a unique ambience of mystery. **Lèvres De Sang** may be seen as the conclusion of this preoccupation, which has haunted both **Le Viol Du Vampire** and **La Vampire Nue**. Corbière and Leroux wrote around the circle of French Decadent writers, among which was Jean Lorrain, the author of this passage from the short story "The Glass Of Blood":

"...It is the governess who has the task of conducting the girl [Rosaria] into the depths; every morning they go down, at five or six o'clock, to the devil's kitchen beneath the rue de Flandre, to an enclosure where the blood is drained from the living calves, to make the white and tender meat.

"And while the young girl makes her descent into that place... La Barina stays here... perfectly tragic in her velvet and lace, mirroring in her mode of dress the snow-whiteness of the narcissi, the frost-whiteness of the tulips and the nacreous whiteness of the irises; here, striking a pose with just a hint of theatricality, she watches. ...and her anguish reaches into the uttermost depths of her soul while she anticipates the first kiss which the child will place upon her lips, as soon as she returns: a kiss which always carries an insipid trace of the taste of blood and a faint hint of that odour which perpetually defiles the rue de Flandre, but which, strangely enough, she does not detest at all – quite the contrary – when it is upon the lips of her beloved Rosaria."

The lurid tale documents how a wealthy aristocratic marquise (La Barina) cures a consumptive young girl's (Rosaria) wax-like pallor, by leading her down to an abattoir to drink blood. The arresting image of a beautiful girl standing in a slaughterhouse germinated into a truly evil

flower, a masterpiece of *amour fou*, **Fascination**. It also serves as an ideal preface to Rollin's artistic output, that of allure and its fatal consequences. Lorrain was perhaps the most decadent of all French writers; his nemesis, like that of Aubrey Beardsley and so many Decadent writers, was tuberculosis. The writer enlisted the help of alternative medicine to prevent the worsening of his illness, using such remedies as ox blood; others, like ether, had hallucinogenic side effects and fuelled, as with Poe and opium, his extravagant literary descents into perversion and sin more profoundly than with any other writer of his day. The above passage is written with an almost fetishistic attention to detail, and the detached sense of timelessness is rominiscent of a Rollin film.

It is not just the aesthetics of a decadent genre that have inspired Rollin, but even more so their philosophy. Rollin's philosophy is essentially Sadean, the same philosophy that cornerstones both the Decadent and Surrealist movements, which have both made a profound impression on Rollin. Baudelaire felt, as did Sade, that sin was a "natural state of human nature" and that "in the act of love there is a great resemblance to torture or a surgical operation", concluding that "one must always come back to Sade, that is to say to natural man, to explain evil". Baudelaire cultivated poetry in themes of the most appalling taste, which is often remarked about Rollin. The ubiquitous *Aurum Film Encyclopedia* notes **Requiem Pour Un Vampire**'s "stylised Sadean sex scenes" and goes onto say that "..the sex scenes look as if they were inserted as autonomous fragments, probably to ensure box office successes". Indeed they were, as Rollin has explained in many interviews, but despite his insistence of his dislike for these scenes, they are filmed with a dubious relish and intensity to rival some of Franco's earlier sado-masochistic chronicles. However, they are not without redeeming features, as the *Aurum* continues: "But within these terms, they are beautifully achieved comic strip nightmares."

LES FILMS A B C et SAM SELSKY présentent
un film de
JEAN ROLLIN
REQUIEM
POUR UN
VAMPIRE
VIERGE
ET
VAMPIRE
MARIE-PIERRE CASTEL
MIREILLE D'ARGENT
PHILIPPE GASTE
LOUISE DHOUR
PAUL BISCIGLIA
MICHEL DELESALLE
eastmancolor
NTERDIT
UX MOINS
E 18 ANS
DIFFUSION MONDIALE: LES FILMS DE OBELIS
DISTRIBUE PAR : LES FILMS DE L'ETOILE /FR

Even *Video Watchdog*'s Tim Lucas admits that "It's nasty and out of character with the surrounding footage, but it also has a ferociously tactile, undeniably sexual appeal, and the culminative image of a bat nestling in female pubic hair is quintessentially Rollin." (Perhaps to be more accurate, it's Rollin paying homage to a quintessential image of Clovis Trouille).

Returning to the abattoir scene in **Fascination**, the sequence is shot in an almost identical manner to one in the first part of Walerian Borowczyk's **Contes Immoraux/Immoral Tales**, based on a story by André Pyere De Mandiargues entitled "The Tide". The sequence in question is where a sixteen-year-old girl anticipates fellating her older cousin on a beach, where long shots are cut with extreme close-ups of the ajar mouth of the girl whilst she runs her finger over her lips. Even if Borowczyk had not filmed the scene six years before, Rollin surely would have invented it. In fact Rollin, in some ways, is rather similar to Borowczyk. They both have their own equally distinctive idiosyncratic style; Borowczyk's seems to have arisen from his background as a brilliant painter and animator, like Rollin having few, if any, cinematic influences whatsoever. Rollin's canvas is often motionless, characters walk in and out of frame, appearing as dots on the horizon, ending in tight unfocused encounters with the audience. The effect is claustrophobic and forms an air of unease between the audience and characters. Rollin utilises the full potential of the medium by synchronising the visuals with an equally extravagant soundtrack, comprising a vast range of musical accompaniments, from the fragmented, disjointed jazz of **Viol** to the angelic wails of **Fascination**. The soundtrack to **Fascination** is very similar to Popol Vuh's in Werner Herzog's somnambulistic **Nosferatu**, despite both of them being released in the same year – "great minds" as they say…

Interestingly, the fleshed-out "Immoral Tale" **La Bête** features the same château as in **Fascination**, and the scenario of the aforementioned film, that of a thief who hides in a château, but no matter how hard he tries cannot bring himself to leave, was a theme similarly explored in Borowczyk's truly amazing **Dr Jekyll Et Les Femmes**.

The locus of these dark fantasies remains a singular poetic image. The lithe female vampire whose coming ruptures the chimes of midnight as she slithers out of a clock in the bridal chamber of a lone virtuous virginal bride, whom she proceeds to seduce, in **Le Frisson Des Vampires**. The scene embodies the archetypes of the sexual sub-conscious; the vampire's lesbianism prises apart the newly weds, her spectre sways the girl to sleep alone on her wedding night, where she can be corrupted. Likewise the girl playing the graveyard-bound piano in **Requiem Pour Un Vampire**, the afore-mentioned scene in **Fascination** and final scene in Rollin's most overtly Oedipal piece, **Lèvres De Sang**, where the protagonist is vampirised by a sister figure in a coffin as it floats off to sea – the image justifying the incestuous relationship between the lovers, as does the Surrealist preoccupation of *amour fou*, that of being loved to death. In a similar vein, the opening sequence to Borowczyk's live-action companion piece to his animated **Les Jeux Des Anges**, **Blanche**, in the words of Philip Strick "spells out the story of **Blanche** for us in just... three cyphers; the fairytale fortress which could easily be the ogre's lair, the white dove fluttering in panic behind wooden bars like innocence over-protected, and the defencelessly nude Blanche herself, an instant target for unpermitted lusts".

Georges Franju, even more so than Luis Buñuel, must be Rollin's primary influence. Rollin met Franju and Buñuel whilst filming his very first shorts; he admired the political anarchism of Buñuel and the poetry of Franju's documentaries. Franju, like Rollin, was deeply influenced by a cinematic style of the past, especially the serials of Feuillade which he lovingly replicated in his **Judex**. Rollin has acknowledged **Judex** as the source for the animal-masked cult in **La Vampire Nue**. Franju and Rollin have also been influenced by German Expressionism, particularly the work of Fritz Lang, which Rollin has paid homage to by referring to **Moonfleet** in several of his films. Franju also shared the classical cinematic urban poetry of Marcel Carné, a style which was revolted against during the emergence of the New Wave when Rollin was starting to make films. Franju and Rollin are always "black and white", never grey. There are virgins and there are vampires. In **Judex** there is the masked, black-garbed villainess, Diana, and Edith Schob's innocent, even celestial, figure. These contrasts are reflected in the expressionist approach to lighting in both of their films. From these images grow films constructed in an inimitably anarchistic, almost improvisational manner, taking a cue from the early crime serials of Feuillade. Feuillade was in fact the sort of commercial filmmaker that was opposed by the avant-garde, as was Rollin, and he fell under similar criticism. Witness Louis Delluc: "**Judex** and **The New Mission Of Judex**, are more serious crimes than those condemned by court martial." Harsher words have been spoken about Rollin for precisely the same reasons. However, Feuillade was – and Rollin probably would have been – greatly favoured by the Surrealists.

Rollin's penchant for his expressionist style, which perhaps climaxes in **Démoniaques**, began whilst working with French psychedelic comic strip artists Phillipe Druillet (and later Caza). The trilogy of **La Vampire Nue**, **Le Frisson Des Vampires** and **Requiem Pour Un Vampire** have the look of a

comic strip, their interiors drowned in colourful spotlights, integrating them into his flat mosaic of cobalt blue and scarlet akin to that of the criminally ignored Mario Bava. Whilst the chaotic collages of Max Ernst and the pop surrealism of Clovis Trouille have made an indelible stamp on earlier Rollin opuses, the languid approach of Paul Delvaux's paintings has suffused the Rollin tableaux after **La Rose De Fer** and **Lèvres De Sang**. While the allusive girl in the abattoir appears to gaze at us infinitesimally, like the girl in the cinema in **Lèvres De Sang**, she appears obtainable only at a price, for sex is equated with death. The ambience in **Lèvres De Sang** and **Fascination** is no longer one of pulp gothic, rather a landscape of silence and emptiness. Rollin's brand of eroticism is generated by combining opposites, the ideal and the obscene. The juxtaposition of religious iconography and blasphemous perversion is a much dwelt-upon theme, from the black mass in **Viol** to the congregation of hooded skeletons at the altar in **Requiem**.

The third "character" in Rollin's films, a castle or château (an notion consolidated by Rollin when he described how the castle in **Le Frisson Des Vampires** was originally intended to "bleed" when the vampires were killed), is repeatedly crammed with antiquarian objects from the past, giving rise to a long-forgotten memory. The most memorable sequence in **The Living Dead Girl** is where the long-deceased Françoise Blanchard phones Marina Piero amidst sentiments of her childhood.

An aesthetic which has constantly plagued Rollin's work is that of women dressed in brilliant white. This can be perceived as either a wedding gown (**Frisson**) or a death shroud (**The Living Dead Girl**); naturally, like Buñuel in **Abismos De Pasión** – his take on *Wuthering Heights* – Rollin unites the two perceptions. In his first film **Viol**, the vampire is wedded in a theatre and then nailed into a coffin with her lover.

As with Surrealists and their literary predecessors, Rollin is fascinated with the *femme fatale*. The Rollin female distinctly conforms to one of the two characters found in vampire literature, whether they be virginal or predatory – beautiful, full of ambiguities and paradoxes which make her all the more alluring. She is told to "stop playing games" at the beginning of **Fascination**, but instead she continues. She's passionate but her love is inaccessible; the final part of **Fascination** elaborates this idea, where a string of female vampires are lined against a wall as if in some amateur wedding photograph, enticing their victim. Lust triumphs over love in the Rollin film. When Elizabeth in **Fascination** reveals her love for Mark, we later learn she desires his blood above anything else, and once she's taken that blood she returns beneath the sapphic gaze of her vampire cult's leader.

Rollin's relationship with his *femme fatales* is as intense as, and comparable to, that of Baudelaire. This philosophy goads accusations of misogyny, but is more a result of sexual unease felt by an artist overwhelmed by desire. Reducing women merely to objects is, after all, a typical Surrealist preoccupation. The sadism in Rollin's films has more in common with the subversion and defiling of dolls in the photographs of Hans Bellmer, than perhaps anyone else working in the genre. But what Rollin has done, for all of his failings, is to have created some of the most arresting images to be captured on film. He is a genuine poet composing in the cinematic medium.

–Daniel Bird

1. Rollin paid tribute to Gaston Leroux in issues 23 and 24 of the horror film journal *Midi/Minuit Fantastique,* in 1970; issue 23 featured a psychedelic sex vampire image from Rollin's **Le Frisson Des Vampires**.

midi/minuit
FANTASTIQUE
n°23

gaston
leroux 1

Automne 1970 - 12 F

Interdit aux moins de 18 ans

LE VIOL DU VAMPIRE

Also known as: **La Reine Des Vampires**
English title: **Rape Of The Vampire**
France, 1968.
Director: Jean Rollin. **Producer:** Sam Selsky, Films ABC. **Writers:** Jean Rollin, Alain Yves
Beaujour. **Cinematography:** Guy Leblond, Antoine Harispe. **Set design:** Alain-Yves
Beaujoue. **Poster design:** Philippe Druillet
Cast: Bernard Letrou, Solange Pradel, Ursule Pauly, Nicole Romain, Catherine Devil,
Jacqueline Sieger, Ariane Sapriel, Eric Yan, Marquis Polho, Alain Beaujour, Olivier Martin,
Barbara Girard, Annie Merlin, Doc Moyle, Marc Pauly, Philippe Druillet, Jean Rollin.

"A first film, a first feature film, that's a little like an announcement of films to come. When I
made **Le Viol** I was not quite sure that I would get the chance to make a second film. Like most
beginners I packed it with as many images and ideas as possible. The result was a sort of
dadaist mess, an incomprehensible serial for the majority of viewers."
–Jean Rollin, *Virgins & Vampires*

Jean Rollin began making films in 1958 with **Les Amours Jaunes**, inspired by a decadent
poem by Tristan Corbière. A sporadic series of short works followed, of which the most notable
are **L'Itinéraire Marin** (1963), an abandoned feature project with script input by Marguerite
Duras, and **Vivre En Espagne** (1964), a documentary on Spain's anti-Franco resistance
movement which was projected at numerous left-wing political gatherings in Paris. It was into this
climate of social unrest and protest that Rollin would eventually unleash his first feature, **Le Viol
Du Vampire**, in 1968 – with surprising results.

The film came about through Rollin's asociation with American film importer/distributor
Sam Selsky, whom he had approached for funding for an unfilmed scenario entitled "Le Dernière
Vampire". Selsky was at that time involved in marketing an old 1943 PRC horror production,
Dead Men Walk, which he had retitled **Le Vampire, Créature Du Diable**. In need of a
suitable short supporting film, Selsky turned to Rollin who came up with the provocative title **Le
Viol Du Vampire**. The film, basically an image-collage derived from Rollin's key influences –
decadent poetry, Surrealism, lurid comic books, and pulp fiction – was shot in black and white
with a cast of crew of friends and family, and largely improvised. Selsky was suitably impressed –
particularly by the results achievd on a modest budget – and quickly decided that the film should
be expanded to feature length. Rollin duly obliged with a "sequel", **Les Femmes Vampires**,
and the two halves were combined.

When the resulting feature was finally released – with unusually high levels of nudity and
blood due to lax censorship regulation of short films (Selsky had cleverly submitted **Le Viol Du
Vampire** and **Les Femmes Vampires** separately, before editing them together) – its virtually
indecipherable plot and deranged imagery caused outrage and antipathy amongst Parisian film
critics and audiences alike. While this vehement reaction came as a shock to Rollin, the positive
outcome was that he and his his film drew so much attention that he found it relatively easy to
raise funding for a follow-up; and so shooting began in 1969 for **La Vampire Nue**, the title
alone consolidating the director's reputation as the prime purveyor of psychedelic sex-vampire
cinema.

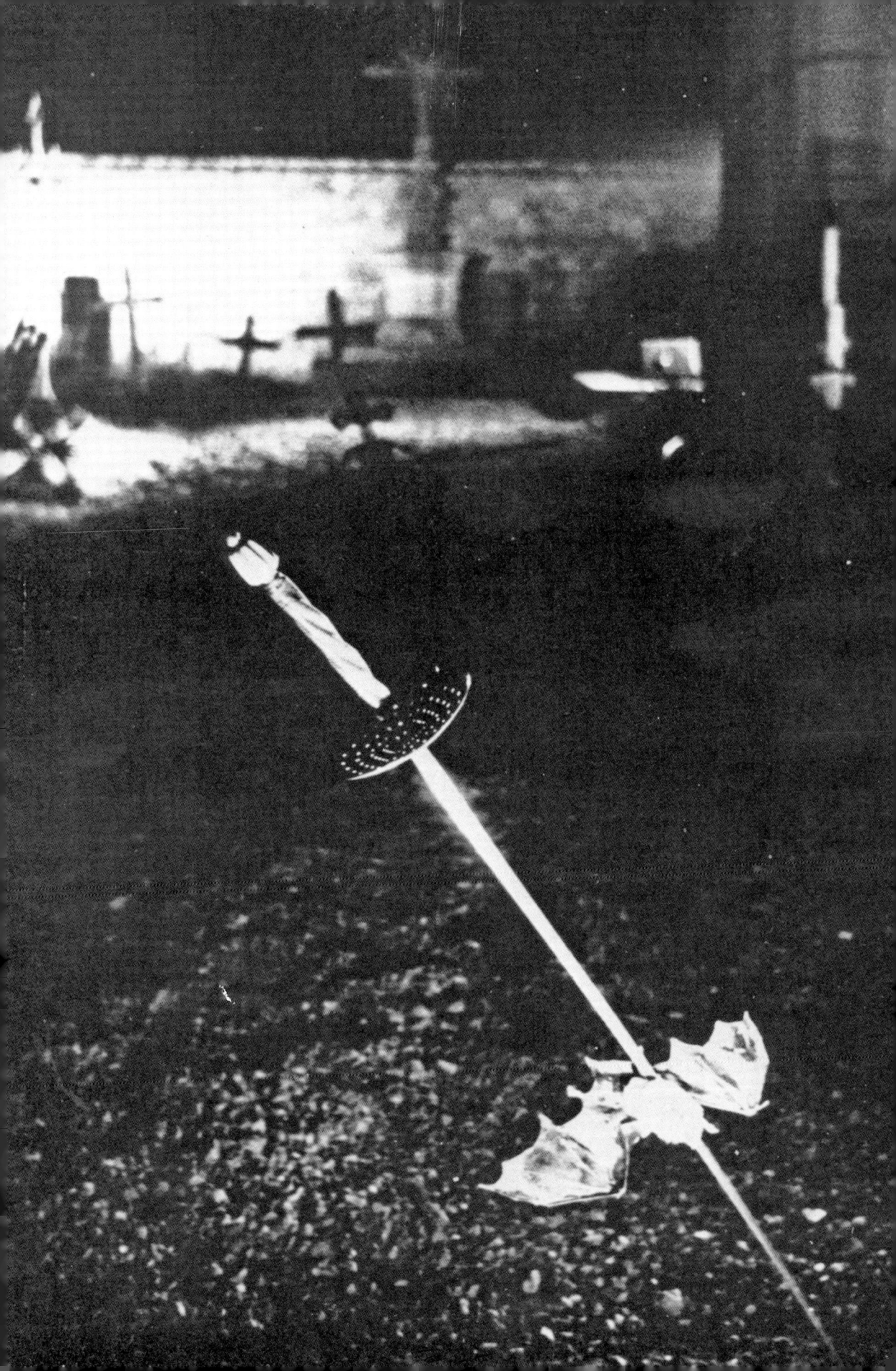

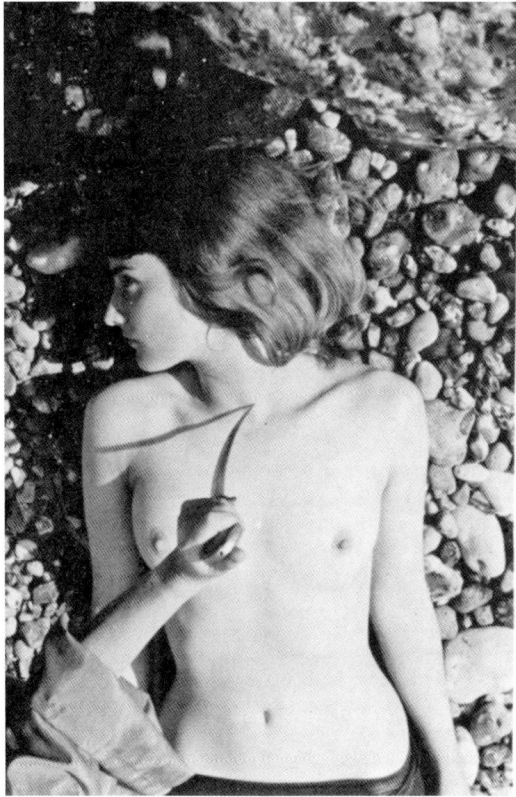

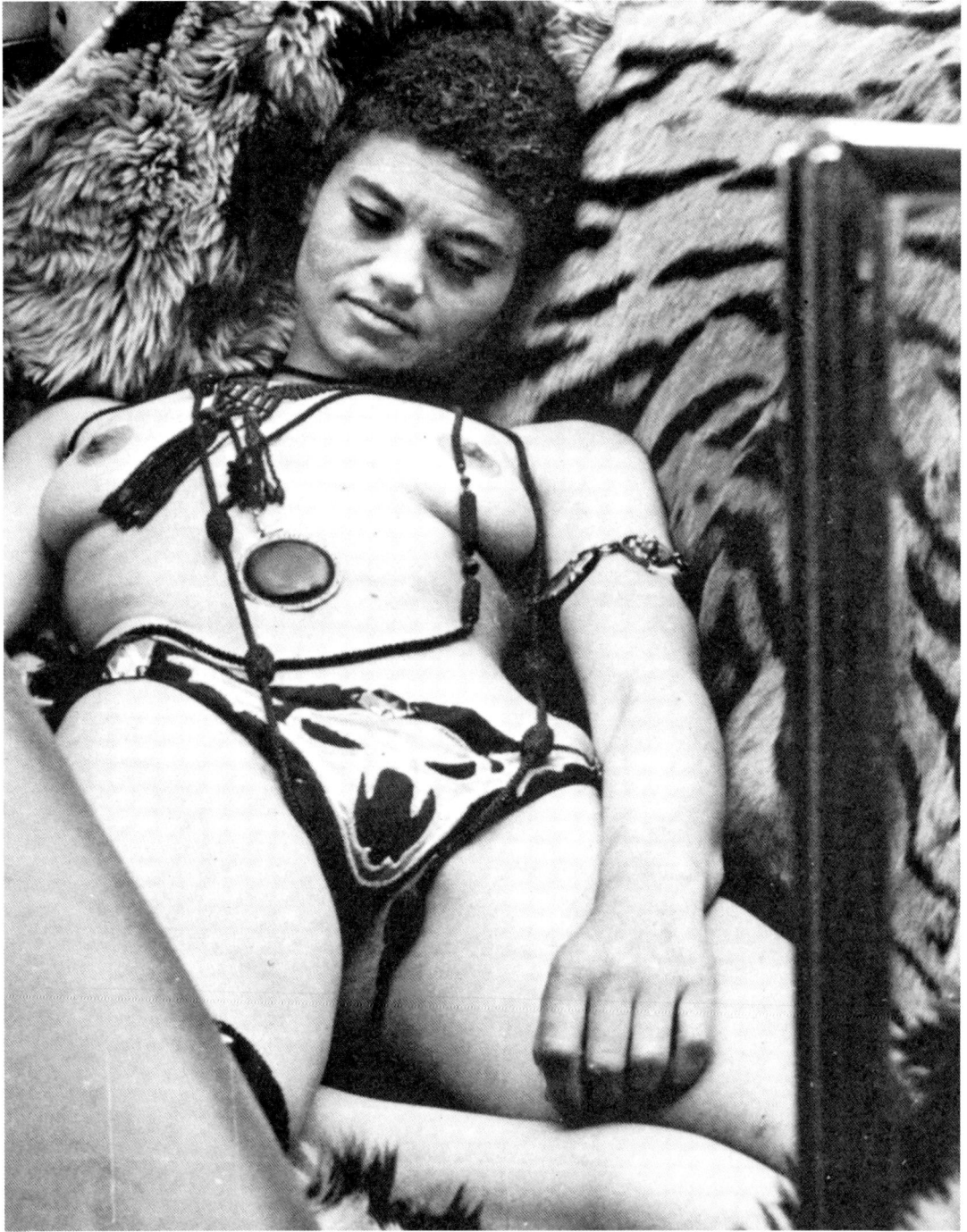

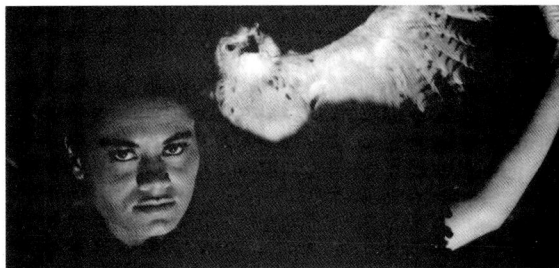

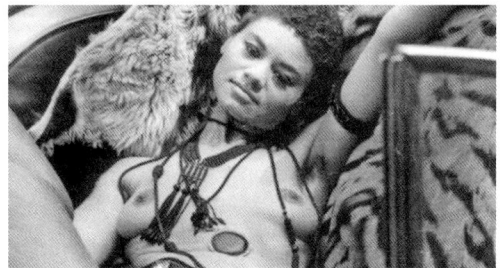

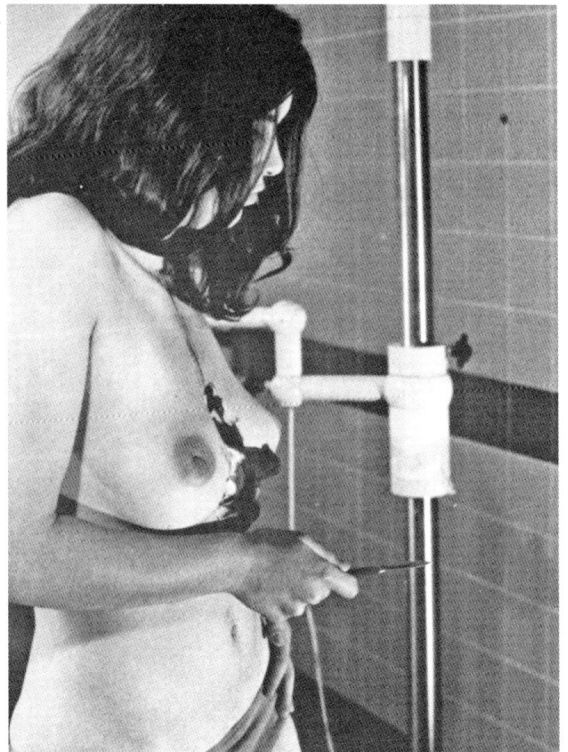

LA VAMPIRE NUE

English title: **The Nude Vampire**
France, 1969.
Director: Jean Rollin. **Producer:** Sam Selsky, Films ABC. **Writers:** Jean Rollin, Serge Moati.
Cinematography: Jean-Jacques Renon. **Set design:** Jio Berk. **Poster design:** Philippe
Druillet
Cast: Christine François, Olivier Martin, Maruice Lemaître, Ly Letrong, Bernard Musson, Cathy
Tricot [Catherine Castel], Pony Tricot [Marie-Pierre Castel], Michel Delahaye, Pascal Fardoulis,
Paul Bisciglia, Nicole Isimat, René Chauffard, Natalie Perrey.

"**La Vampire Nue** was conceived as a mystery film. There were a few strong ideas (not very
well executed, I realise now) like the hidden young girl who has never seen a human being; the
guru type played by my friend Michel Dalahaye; the final theatrical revelation: the vampires
aren't vampires... they are mutants; a scene shot on my "fetish" beach at Pourville."
–Jean Rollin, *Virgins & Vampires*

Produced by Sam Selsky and shot in colour, **La Vampire Nue** features outlandish design,
costumes and visual stylings by Jio Berk, a Belgian underground artist. The plot – conceived by
Rollin as a structure of accumulating enigma – concerns The Master, a mysterious figure who lives
in an opulent castle with two twin female acolytes (played by future Rollin regulars, the Castel
sisters). A strange suicide cult revolves around The Master, with devotees willing to give their own
blood to keep him alive. Hoods, animal masks, medical experiments and weird ceremonies add
to the atmosphere of pulp delirium. Through this bizarre set-up wanders a full-breasted, blood-
drinking young girl (Christine François), naked beneath a diaphanous orange gown and
apparently resurrected from the grave; the wonders she encounters include a naked black girl
and a trio of go-go dancers in psychedelic garb and coloured wigs, with metal spikes protruding
from their nipples. Rollin's SF-tinged semi-dénouement reveals the strange cult to be mutants from
another dimension, only augmenting the film's aura of unreality.

Sadly, initial screenings of **La Vampire Nue** were met with a general mix of
incomprehension and derision, and it was not a great commercial success – a situation
exacerbated by Rollin going over-budget during production.

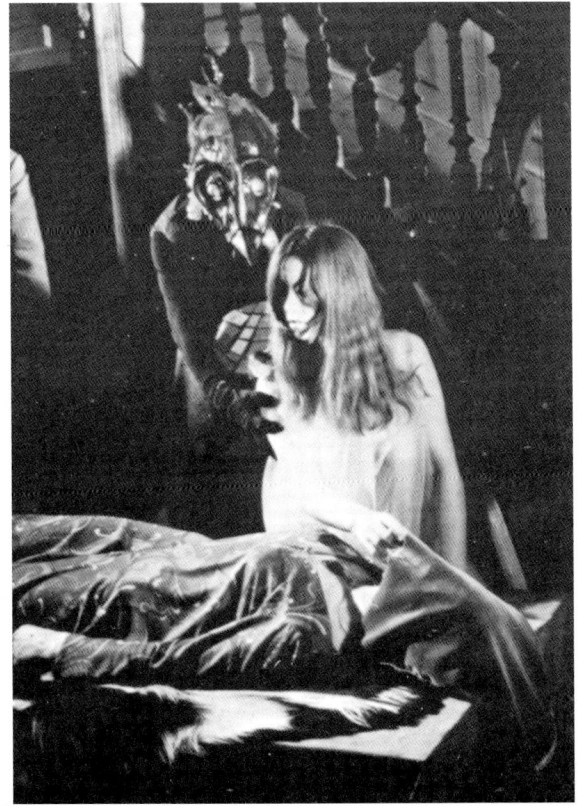

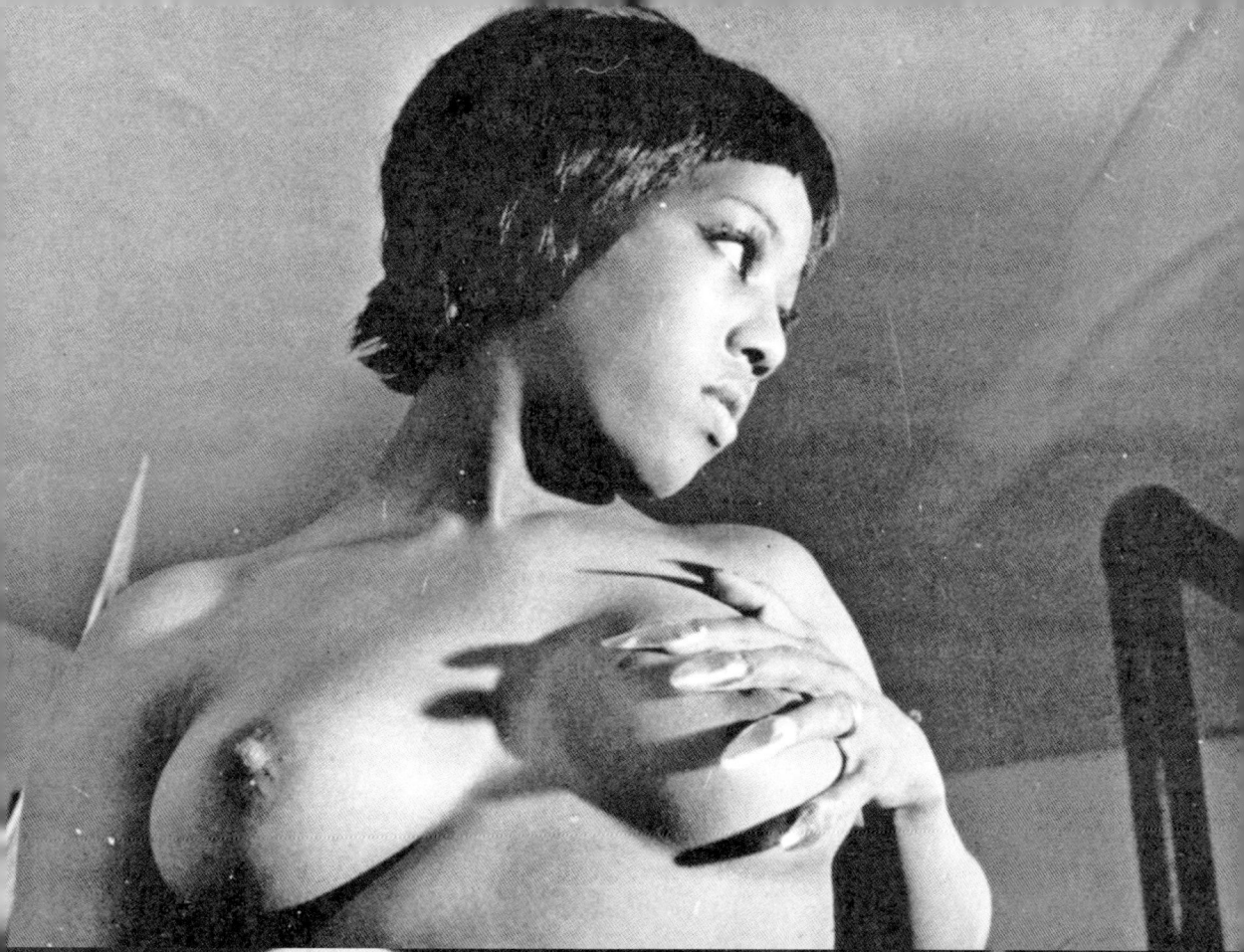

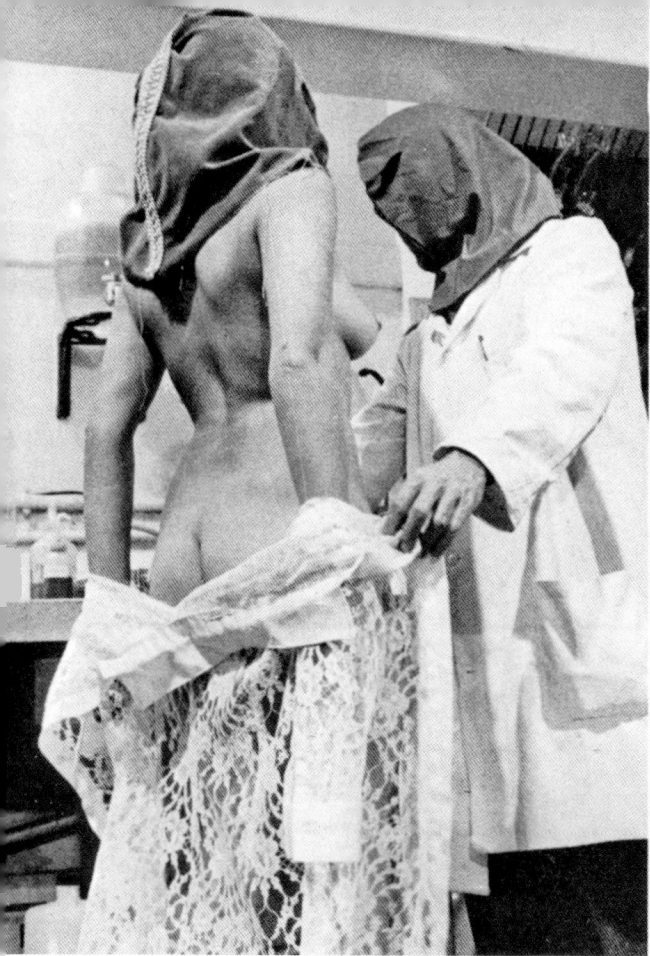
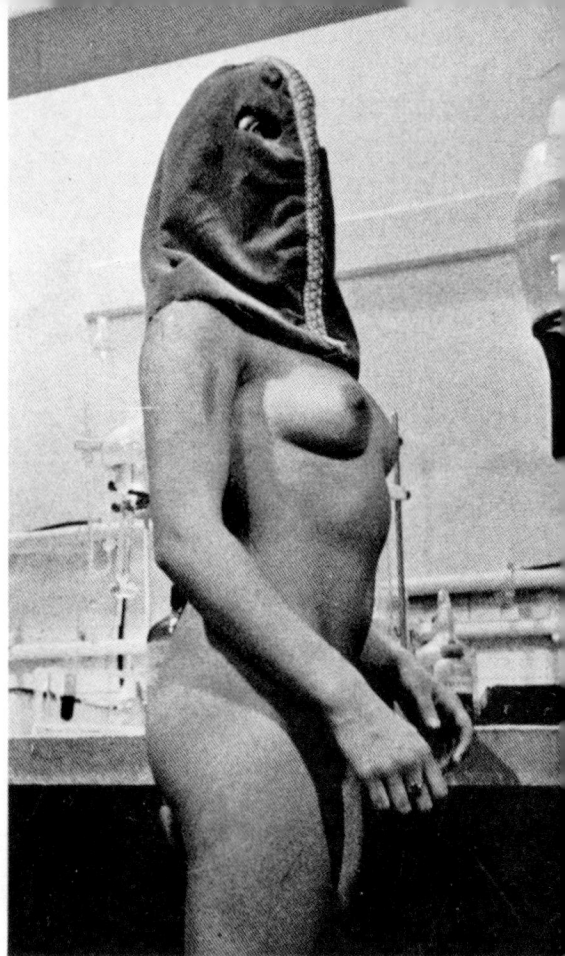

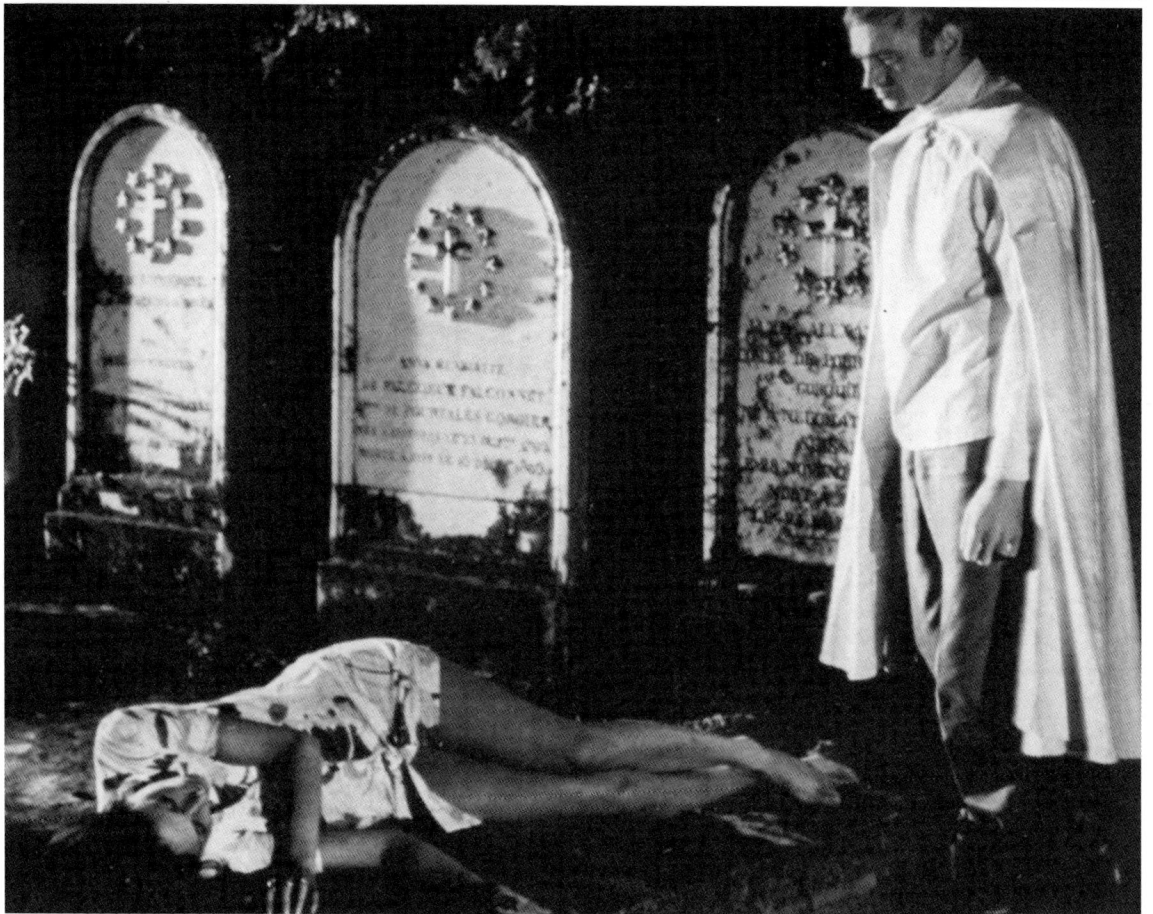

LE FRISSON DES VAMPIRES

English titles: **Sex And The Vampire**; **Terror Of The Vampires**
France, 1970.
Director: Jean Rollin. **Producer:** Les Films Modernes. **Writer:** Jean Rollin.
Cinematography: Jean-Jacques Renon. **Set design:** Michel Delesalle. **Poster design:**
Philippe Druillet. **Music:** Acanthus.
Cast: Sandra Julien, Jean-Marie Durand, Michel Delahaye, Jacques Robiolles, Marie-Piere
Castel, Kuelan Herca, Dominique.

"With a deliberately surrealist look *à la* Paul Delvaux I indulged myself with certain twists. A
chaste female nude (one of the Castel twins, Pony) appearing motionless in strange locations:
in a ruins overgrown with vegetation; on a stone staircase leading to nowhere; atop a tower
laughing; standing at the bend of a corridor, etc. All the things that I have been reproached for,
my visual ticks, were there: candelabras, transparent veils, cemeteries at night, chaste nudity,
ruins and eery lighting..."
–Jean Rollin, *Virgins & Vampires*

Produced by Monique Natan, **Le Frisson Des Vampires** stars sex-film actress Sandra Julien
alongside the mysterious Dominique, who plays a lesbian or bisexual vampire adorned with
chains. In one scene she emerges mysteriously and half-naked from within a grandfather clock,
a shot now regarded as perhaps *the* classic Rollin image, an encapsulation of his surrealistic
vision. Once again Rollin utilised his stock gothic iconography to brilliant effect, aided by multi-
coloured lighting and gel filters, and came up with his most commercial work to date.

Other characters in the film include two hippy-type vampire castle-dwellers, and a pair
of seemingly lost orphan girls – the latter to become a defining trope of Rollin's cinema. The girls
(played by Pony Castel and the East Asian Kuelan Herca), clad in see-through gowns, wander
around clutching candelabras while Dominique feeds on the naked Julien and haunts the castle
cemetery.

Also of note is the film's psych-prog soundtrack, provided by a group of "high school
students" named Acanthus, which adds to the overall phantasmagoric effect of this hallucinatory
sex-horror film trip.

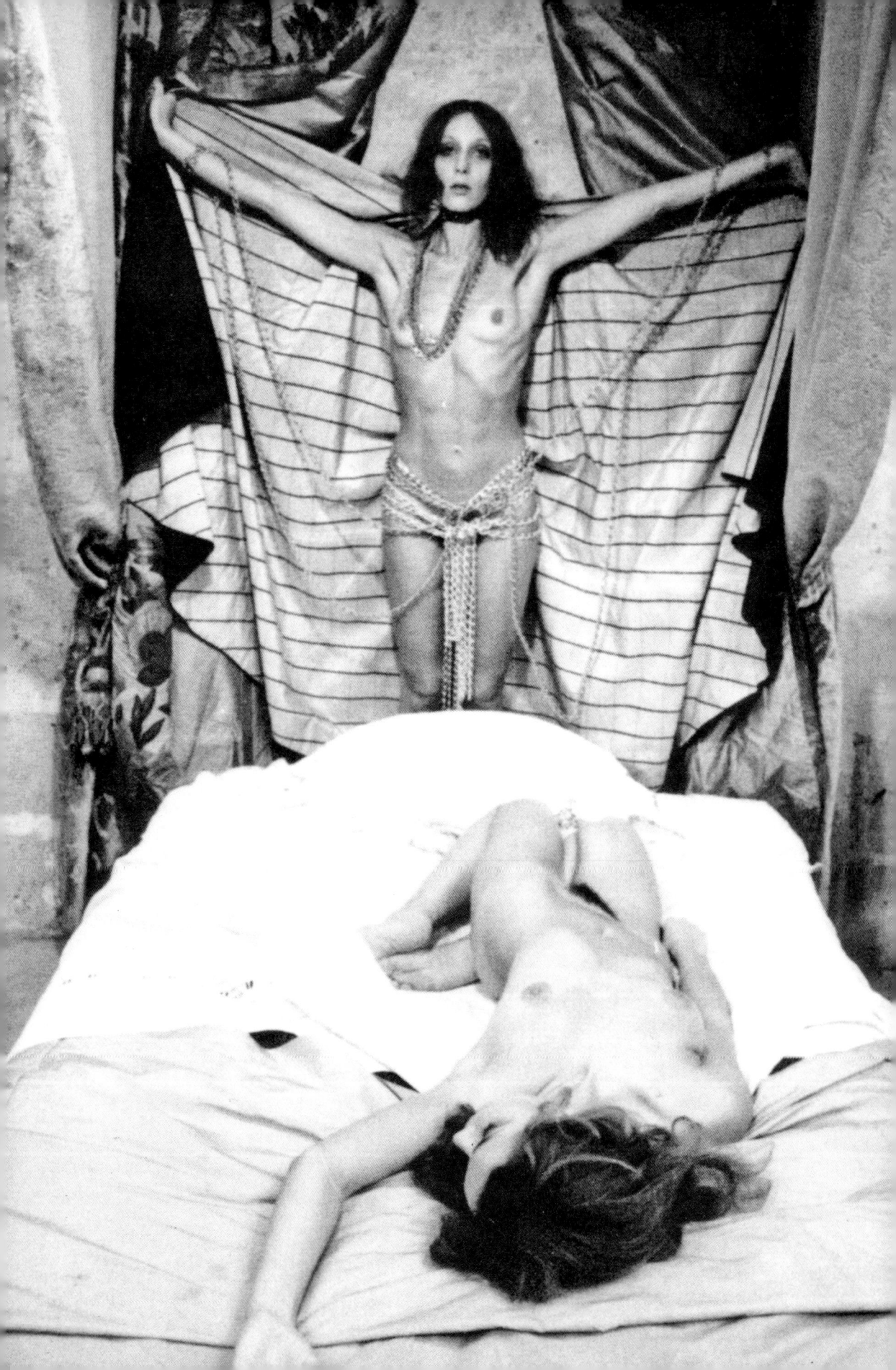

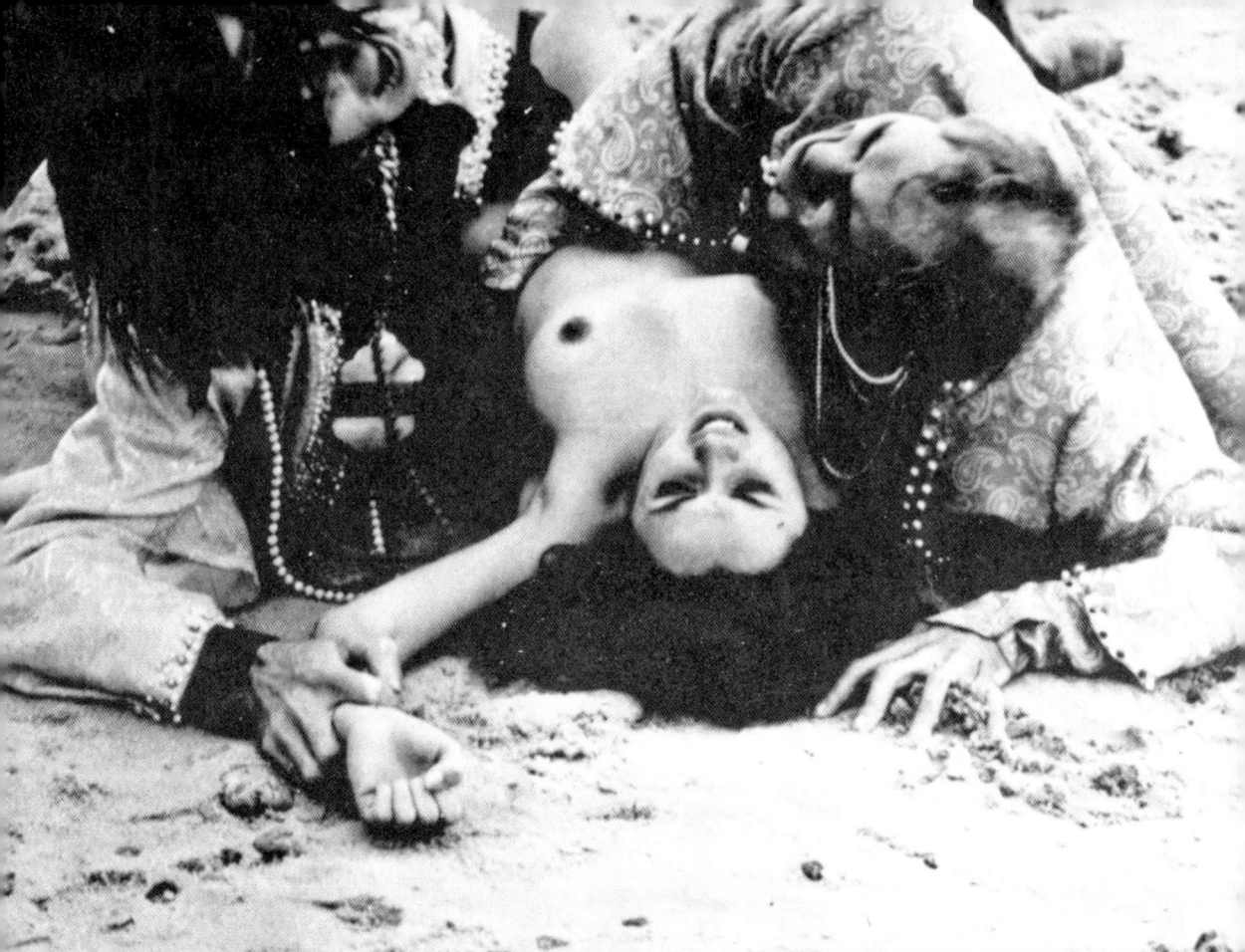

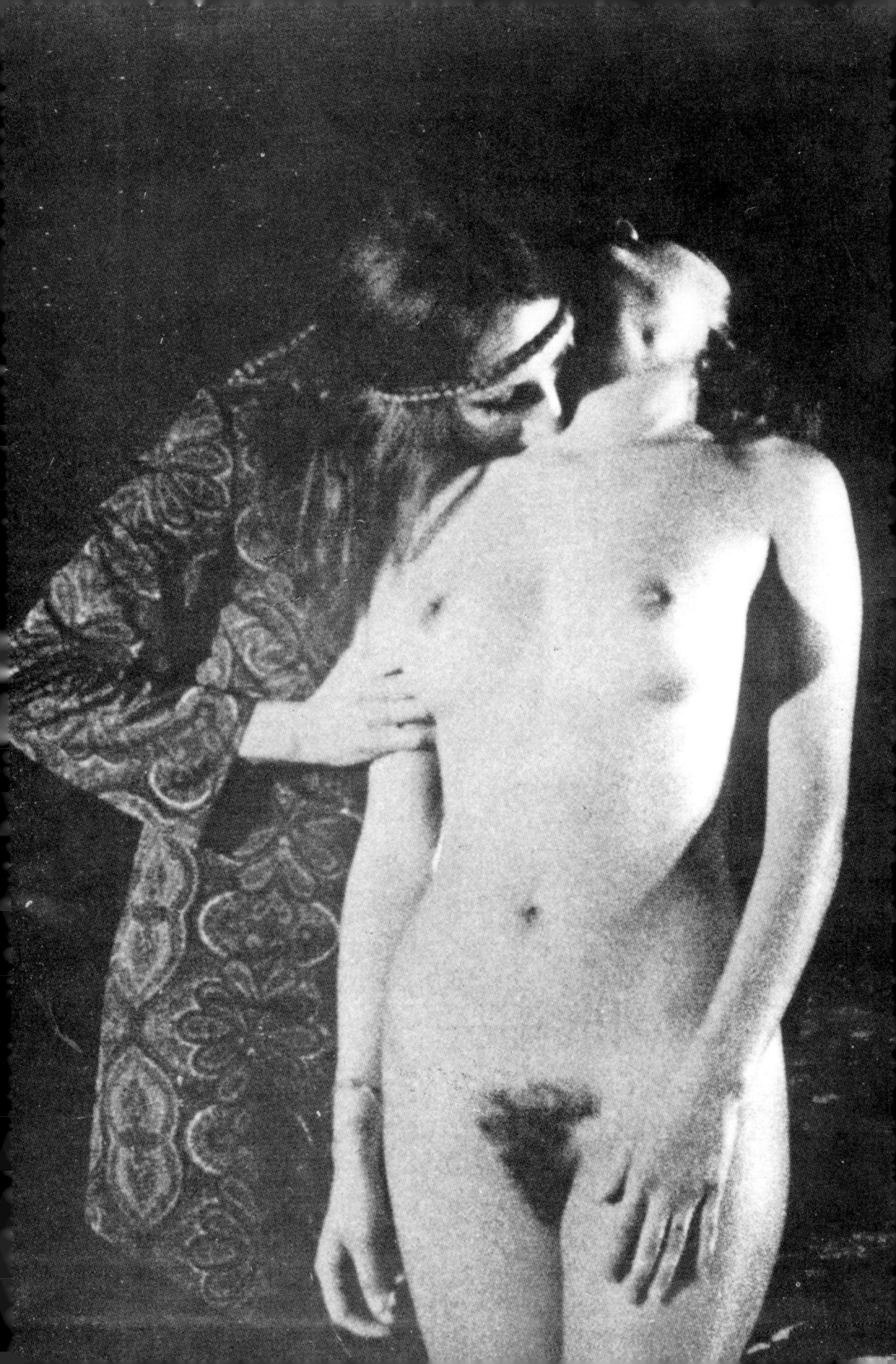

REQUIEM POUR UN VAMPIRE

Also known as: **Vierges Et Vampires**
English titles: **Requiem For A Vampire**; **Caged Virgins**
France, 1971.
Director: Jean Rollin. **Producer:** Sam Selsky, Films ABC. **Writer:** Jean Rollin.
Cinematography: Renan Polles. **Set design:** Michel Delesalle.
Cast: Marie- Pierre Castel, Mireille Dargent, Philippe Gaste, Dominique, Louise Dhour, Michel Delesalle, Paul Bisciglia, Michel François, Antoine Mausin, Dominique Toussaint, Jean-Noel Delamarre.

"I was used to the critics' insults, the public outcry, and I started shooting for my personal pleasure exclusively since the others had rejected me. **Requiem** is an attempt to simplify the structure of a film to the extreme."
–Jean Rollin, *Virgins & Vampires*

Once again produced by Sam Selsky, **Requiem Pour Un Vampire** begins with two girls in a speeding car dressed as clowns, on the run from an unexplained pursuer. The film progresses from image to image, situation to situation, in an ever-building enigma almost completely devoid of dialogue, for the first 40 minutes. The two girls end up in a ruined castle, get naked, are chained and whipped, and are stalked by a male and female vampire. The female plays organ in a chapel of hooded skeletons; the male is apprently the last of his kind, and looking for victims by which to propagate his dying race. Some of the nude/sexual scenes in the film border on SM, and were apparently ramped up at the request of the film's backers.

Requiem Pour Un Vampire, the culmination of Rollin's opening film quartet, once more brought together his personal fetishes – the pair of runaway/lost girls (one dark, one fair); the ruined château haunted by vampires; clowns, nudity, skulls and skeletons, candelabra, dungeons, graveyards – and married them to a story marked by escalating mystery and visual delirium. It stands as his first psychedelic sex-horror masterpiece.

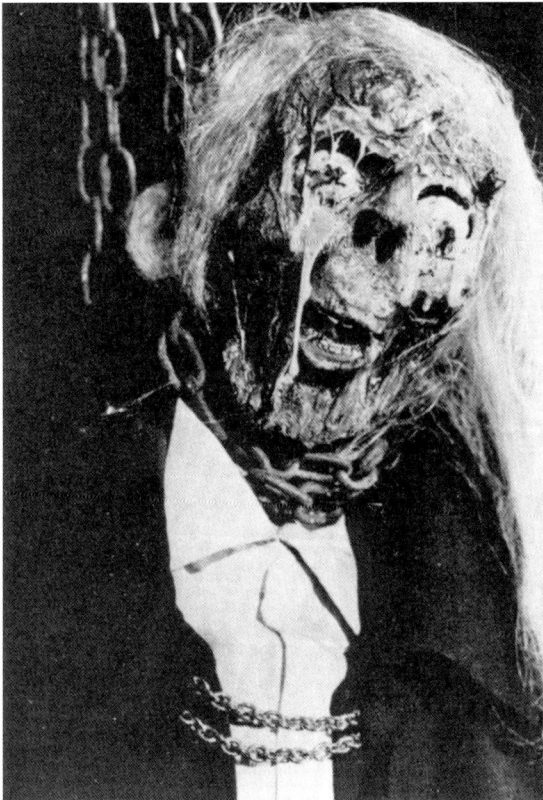

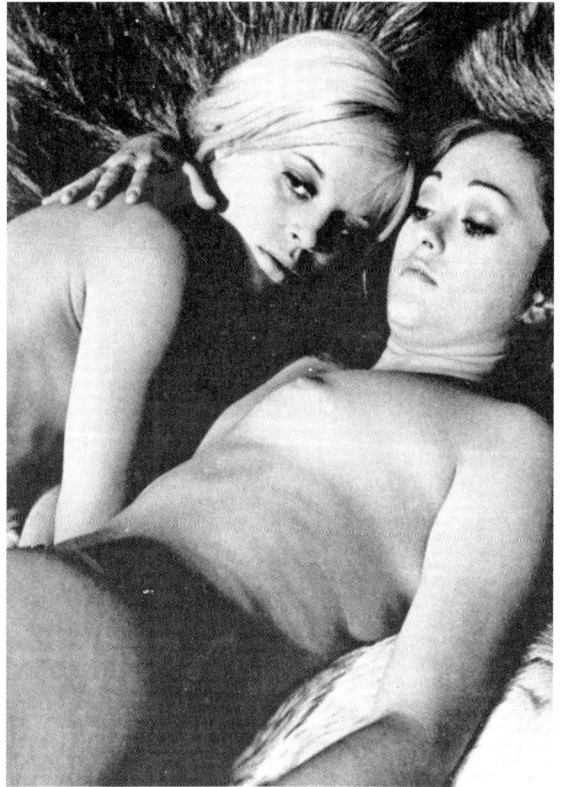

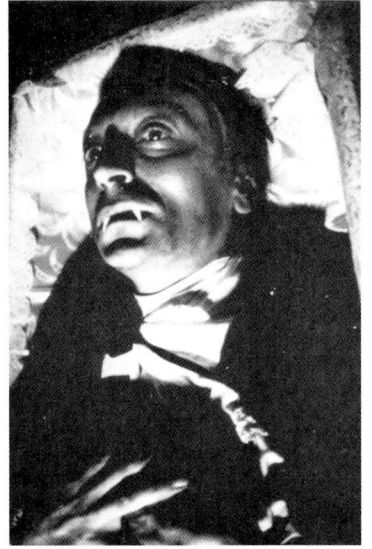

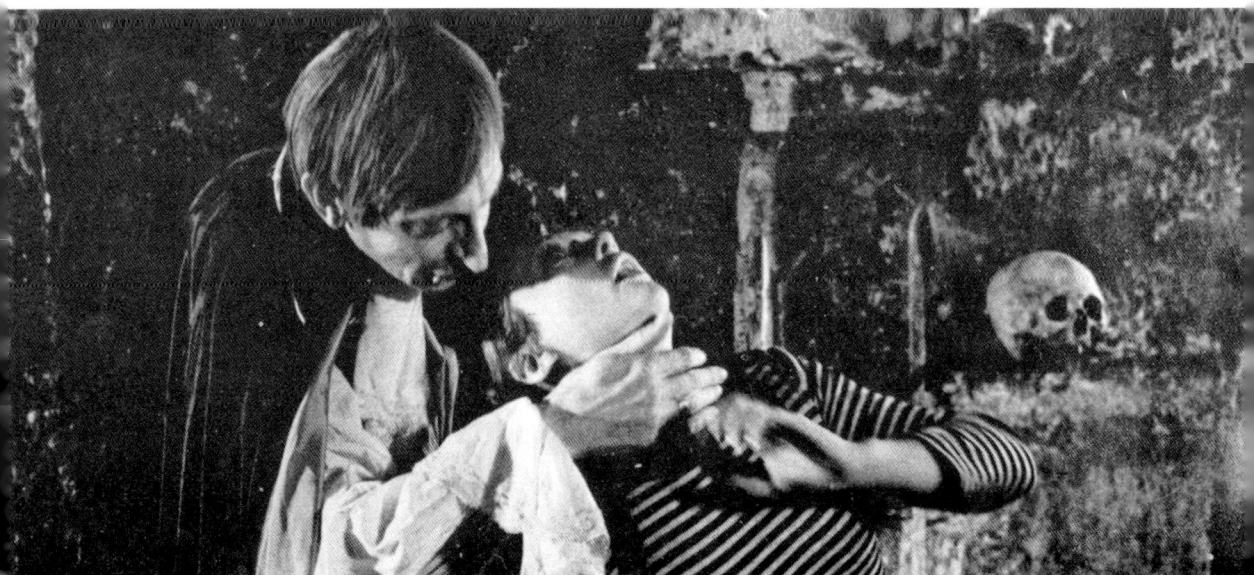

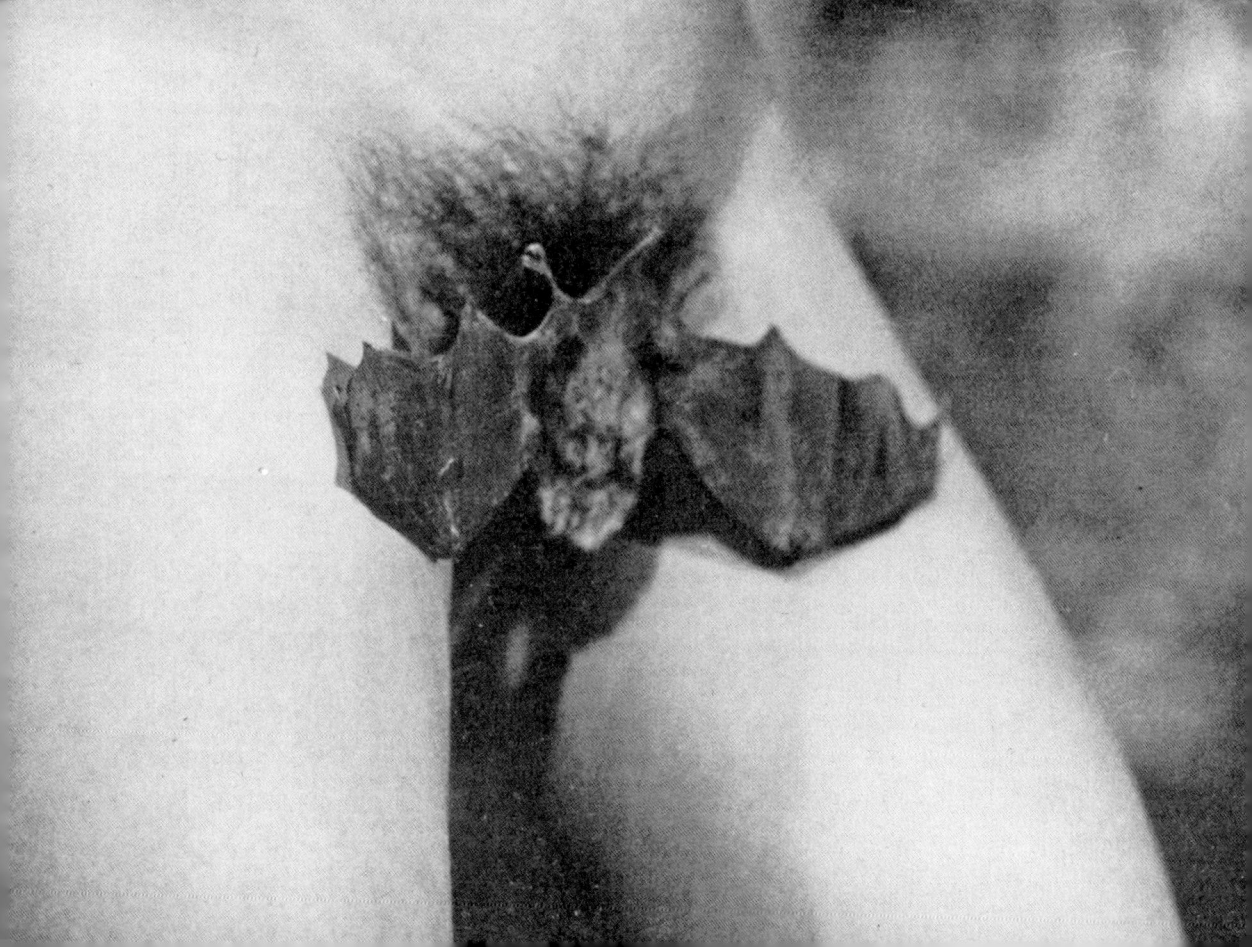

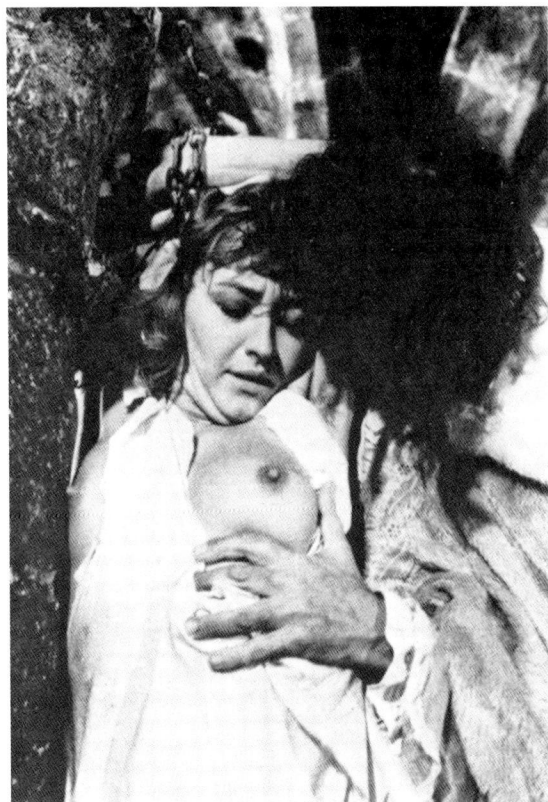

A FILMOGRAPHY

1. THE EARLY FILMS (1958-1965)

LES AMOURS JAUNES
(France, 1958)
Director: Jean Rollin

CIEL DE CUIVRE
(France, 1960)
Director: Jean Rollin.
Short film.

UN CHEVAL POUR DEUX
(France, 1962)
Director: Jean-Marc Thibault; **Assistant director:** Jean Rollin.

L'ITINÉRAIRE MARIN
(France, 1963)
Director: Jean Rollin.
Unfinished feature.

VIVRE EN ESPAGNE
(France, 1964)
Director: Jean Rollin
Short documentary film.

LE PAYS LOIN
(France, 1965)
Director: Jean Rollin.
Short film.

2. THE GOLDEN AGE (1968-83)

LE VIOL DU VAMPIRE
(France, 1968)
Director: Jean Rollin.

LA VAMPIRE NUE
(France, 1969)
Director: Jean Rollin.

LE FRISSON DES VAMPIRES

(France, 1970)
Director: Jean Rollin.

REQUIEM POUR UN VAMPIRE

(France, 1971)
Director: Jean Rollin.

LA ROSE DE FER

(France, 1972)
Original title: **La Nuit Du Cimitière**.
Director: Jean Rollin.

LES DÉMONIAQUES

(France, 1973)
Original titles: **Les Diablesses; Deux Vierges Pour Satan**.
Director: Jean Rollin.

LÈVRES DE SANG

Original title: **Jennifer**.
(France, 1974)
Director: Jean Rollin.

PHANTASMES

(France, 1975)
English title: **The Seduction Of Amy**.
Director: Jean Rollin.

LES RAISINS DE LA MORT
(France, 1978)
Original title: **Pesticide.**
English title: **Grapes Of Death.**
Director: Jean Rollin.

FASCINATION
(France, 1979)
Director: Jean Rollin.

LA NUIT DES TRAQUÉES
(France, 1980)
Director: Jean Rollin.

LE LAC DES MORTS-VIVANTS
(France/Spain, 1980)
Spanish title: **El Lago De Los Muertos Vivientes.**
English title: **Zombie Lake.**
Director: Jean Rollin (as J.A. Lazar).

LES ÉCHAPPÉES
(France, 1981)
Original title: **Les Meurtrières.**
Alternative title: **Les Paumées Du Petit Matin.**
English title: **The Runaways.**
Director: Jean Rollin.

LA MORTE VIVANTE
(France, 1982)
English title: **The Living Dead Girl.**
Director: Jean Rollin.

LES TROTTOIRS DE BANGKOK
(France, 1983)
Alternative title: **Bangkok Interdit**.
Director: Jean Rollin.

3. THE PORNO FILMS (1973-82)

JEUNES FILLES IMPUDIQUES
(France, 1973)
English title: **Schoolgirl Hitchhikers**.
Director: Jean Rollin (as Michel Gentil).

TOUT LE MONDE IL EN A DEUX
(France, 1974)
Alternative title (hardcore version): **Bacchanales Sexuelles**.
Director: Jean Rollin (as Michel Gentil).

DOUCES PÉNÉTRATIONS
(France, 1975)
Alternative title: **La Romancière Lubrique**.
Director: Jean Rollin (as Michel Gentil).

SUCE MOI VAMPIRE
(France, 1975)
English title: **Suck Me Vampire**.
An edited version of **Lèvres De Sang**, with hardcore inserts.
Director: Jean Rollin (as Michel Gand).

LA COMTESSE IXE
(France, 1976)
Alternative title: **Suceurs Chaudes**.
Director: Jean Rollin (as Michel Gentil).

HARD PENETRATION
(France, 1976)
Director: Jean Rollin (as Michel Gentil).

VIBRATIONS SEXUELLES
(France, 1976)
Director: Jean Rollin (as Michel Gentil).

APOTHEOSE PORNO
(France, 1976)
Director: Jean Rollin (as Michel Gand).

SAUTE-MOI DESSUS
(France, 1977)
Director: Jean Rollin (as Michel Gentil).

LÈVRES ENTROUVERTES
(France, 1977)
Alternative title: **Monique: Lèvres Entrouvertes Pour Sexe Chaud**.
Director: Jean Rollin (as Michel Gentil).

POSITIONS DANOISES
(France, 1977)
Director: Jean Rollin (as Michel Gentil).

DISCOSEX
(France, 1977)
Director: Jean Rollin (as Robert Xavier).

PETITES PENSIONNAIRES IMPUDIQUES
(France, 1978)
Director: Jean Rollin (as Michel Gentil).

REMPLISSEZ-MOI... LES TROIS TROUS
(France, 1978)
Director: Jean Rollin (as Robert Xavier).

PULSIONS SECRÈTES
(France, 1978)
Director: Jean Rollin (as Robert Xavier).

HYPERPÉNÉTRATIONS
(France, 1978)
Director: Jean Rollin (as Robert Xavier).

PÉNÉTRATIONS VICIEUSES
(France, 1979)
Director: Jean Rollin (as Michel Gentil).

GAMINES EN CHALEUR
(France, 1979)
Director: Jean Rollin (as Robert Xavier).

BOUCHES LASCIVES ET PORNO
(France, 1979)
Director: Jean Rollin (as Robert Xavier).

INTRODUCTIONS PERVERSES

(France, 1979)
Director: Jean Rollin (as Michel Gentil).

RÊVES DE SEXES

(France, 1981)
Director: Jean Rollin (as Robert Xavier).

SODOMANIE

(France, 1982)
Director: Jean Rollin (as Robert Xavier).

FOLIES ANALES

(France, 1982)
Director: Jean Rollin (as Robert Xavier).

4. THE LATE FILMS (1991-2010)

PERDUES DANS NEW YORK

(France, 1991)
English title: **Lost In New York**.
Director: Jean Rollin.

KILLING CAR

(France, 1993)
Original title: **La Femme Dangereuse**.
Director: Jean Rollin.

LES DEUX ORPHELINES VAMPIRES

(France, 1995)
English title: **Two Orphan Vampires**.
Director: Jean Rollin.

LA FINANCÉE DE DRACULA

(France, 2002)
Director: Jean Rollin.

LA NUIT DES HORLOGES

(France, 2007)
Director: Jean Rollin.

LE MASQUE DE LA MÉDUSE

(France, 2010)
Director: Jean Rollin.

5. MISCELLANEOUS

UNE VIERGE CHEZ LES MORTS VIVANTS
(France/Italy/Belgium, 1980)
Original title: **Christina, Princesse De L'Érotisme** (1973)
English title: **A Virgin Among The Living Dead**.
Director: Jesus Franco.
Jean Rollin shot additional zombie/dream footage for Eurociné's re-edited re-release.

NE PRENDS PAS LES POULETS POUR DES PIGEONS
(France, 1985)
Directors: Jean Rollin (as Michel Gentil), Jean-Claude Benhamou.

EMANUELLE 6
(France, 1988)
Director: Bruno Zincone.
Jean Rollin wrote the script and also shot additional scenes.

À LA POURSUITE DE BARBARA
(France/Switzerland, 1990)
English title: **Chasing Barbara**.
Director: Jesus Franco.
Jean Rollin shot additional "jungle" scenes for Eurociné's re-edit of old Franco footage.

LE PARFUM DE MATHILDE
(France, 1994)
Directors: Marc Dorcel, Jean Rollin (uncredited).
Rollin wrote the film scenario and also directed some scenes.

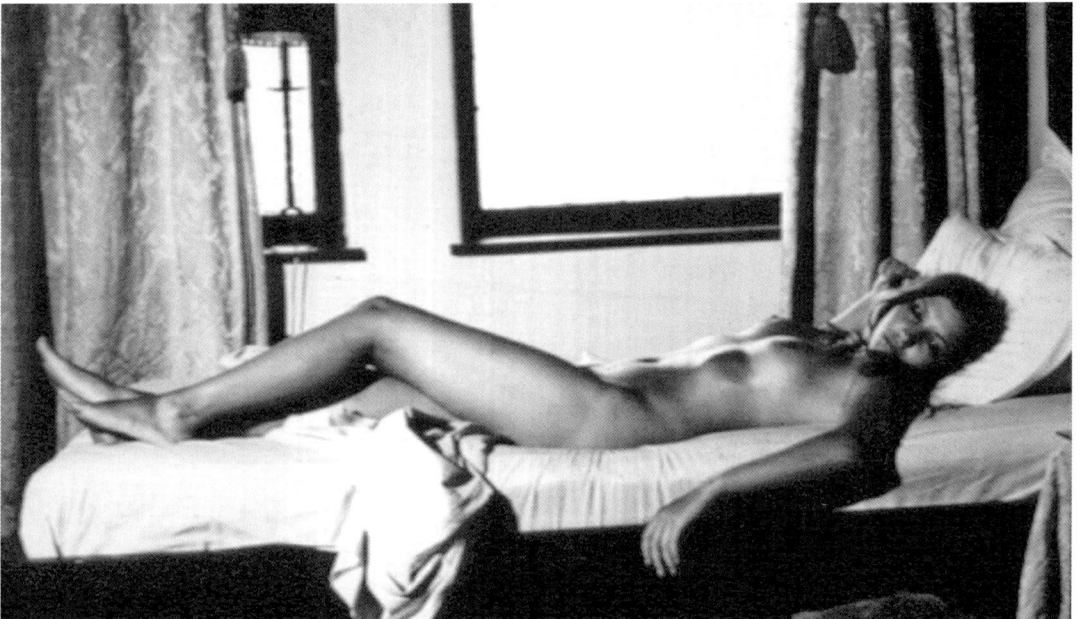

JEAN ROLLIN 1938-2010

AN INTERVIEW WITH JEAN ROLLIN

"A grandfather clock is of no interest – a vampire woman getting out of this clock at midnight, that's me!"
—Jean Rollin

"Dreams and life – it's the same thing; or else it's not worth living."
—From Marcel Carné's *Les Enfants Du Paradis* (1945)

As any viewer who is acquainted with **Le Frisson Des Vampires** in the former case, or *any* of Rollin's surrealist fantasies (and that's basically his whole *oeuvre*!) in the latter case will testify, the above quotations encapsulate Rollin's filmic *raison d'être*, symbolised in his kaleidoscopic costumes and props, decadent characters and nebulous romanticism.

Whilst the Frenchman's early career focused on his now trademark vampire sex "epics" such as **Le Viol Du Vampire**, **La Vampire Nue** and **Requiem Pour Un Vampire**, and encompassed moulding corpses in **Zombie Lake**, masturbatory couplings in **Hard Penetrations** and grotesque gore in **Les Raisins De La Mort**, recent years have been somewhat less than vintage for the mercurial Rollin.

However, vampires make an overdue return with the release of **Les Deux Orphelines Vampires (Little Orphan Vampires)** in 1996 – Rollin's first vampire film for some 10 years.

The master's well-documented love of the old French magazine serials or *feuilletons* shines through, with the film being the first to be adapted from his long line of successful *romans de gare* (station novels) – a unique brand of French "pulp fiction" – which also includes *Anissa*, *Les Voyageuses*, *Les Pillardes* and *Les Incendiares* in this particular vampire novel series.

With **Les Deux Orphelines Vampires**, Rollin revisits his obligatory two female vampire leads – named Louise and Henriette here – and favoured gothic graveyard milieu as the duo of blind vampires ("clack, clack, clack, clack went the two white sticks") await nightfall when their sight (and more importantly, their appetite for blood) returns and they seek out new victims.

The vamps, with their dual personalities alternating effortlessly between good and evil, mirror the equally diverse nature of those Sadean characters Justine and Juliette, a coincidence not lost on Rollin to be sure.

Having tracked down the ubiquitous Rollin, here follows our lengthy dialogue:

You have stated that the poet Corbière and the artists Druillet and Trouille are among those who have inspired your work – in what way?

Corbière was a poet of the sea. And the sea is most important to me. My first short film was an evocation of Corbière on a beach near Dieppe. I was young, no money, no material etc. But I was there, on that strange beach covered in stones, deserted, with just the *falaise* and the seagulls. And in my mind, I said: "One day I'll come back here with all the possibilities for a real shoot." For me, now, after six or seven films shot on that beach, it is mixed with the remembrance of Corbière. Druillet has nothing to do with my work, he is just a friend. After the shooting of **Le Viol Du Vampire** I asked all my friends who can take a pencil to do an image for the poster. Druillet brought [an image] which immediately became the film's poster. Clovis Trouille paints, I think, as I film. When I see some of his

CLOVIS

paintings, it seems to me that they could be photos from one of my films. The same strange arrangements of the elements, romantic-expressionist protagonists, expression of the imagination. As for Magritte, Trouille paints people and objects in a realistic, ultra-realistic manner. It's the arrangement between the elements which forms the surrealist way. Paintings like *Stigma Diaboli*, *La Violée Du Vaisseau Fantôme* ["The Raped Girl From The Haunted Ship" – could be the title from a Rollin film!], *L'Heure Du Sortilège* and so on could absolutely be images from my mind and my films. They are part of the "mystery of the imagination" I like so much. If you look at a painting like *Mon Tombeau* [My Tomb] it can recall many images from **Le Viol**, **Le Frisson** or **Requiem**.

What influence did the likes of Georges Franju and Luis Buñuel have on your career?

It's the same kind. Buñuel shot visions like Trouille did paintings, or Magritte. We can take some images off for film, those images speak for themselves. They are independent of the story, they are the voice of Buñuel himself. So, in a film so banal in appearance like **Susana** or even **El**, everything is shown by the vision of the artist. Personally, I am jealous of an extraordinary vision I saw in one of Buñuel's last French films, I don't remember which one but: a man closes a coffin, and some gold hairs from the dead girl inside are visible. Such imagery leaves me full of exaltation. There are many such images in Buñuel films. Franju is the author of the greatest film of the genre, **Les Yeux Sans Visage**. Perfection of the script, of the actors, of the light, of everything. I was haunted during many, many years by the end, Edith Scob walking in the park with her face covered by the white mask, and the white birds and that music… I have tried to find that atmosphere of dream, poetry and madness in many of my films. Same reflections about **Judex**. It's a serial, like a serial. For me, where the cinema is near the surrealist poetry, near the primitive mind of childhood, it is the serial. My remembrance as a child is of the serials I saw after school every Wednesday – **Zorro Fighting Legion**, **Mysterious Docteur Satan**, **G-Men Versus The Black Dragon**, etc. I think I personally have shot two serials: **Viol Du Vampire** and **Les Trottoirs De Bangkok**. Here a critic said; "Rollin has done with **Bangkok**, the same film as his first one, **Le Viol**, twenty-five years after." And it's true! **Bangkok** is a kind of "Fu-Manchu" and the film was improvised to a great degree like **Le Viol**. When I was shooting it, I was in the same mind that I was for **Le Viol**. I was twenty years old again!

*Your first fantasy film **Le Viol Du Vampire** was considered daring for the time and released during a turbulent period in French history – in what way did this film and the critical reaction to it, shape your future career?*

Le Viol was a terrible scandal here in Paris. People were really mad when they saw it. In Pigalle, they threw things at the screen. The principal reason was that nobody could understand the story. But there *is* a story, I swear it! Now, after such a long time, I think the principal reason is that the film was supposed to be a vampire story. The audience knew only Hammer's vampires and my film disturbed their classical idea of what such a film had to be. And outside it was the revolution, so people were able to exteriorise themselves. The scandal was a terrible surprise for me. I didn't know that I had made such a "bizarre" picture. For me, it was so simple! In all the country, throughout France, the film was a scandal. In my area, a little village, the priest said to his audience in church that they must not see the film on release at their local cinema... I was the devil. And even the fans of such films were disillusioned and the critics wrote horrors about me. A great newspaper, *Le Figaro*, wrote: "this film is certainly made by a group of drunk people, probably medical students. It's a joke". I thought that my career was finished. But many people came to see *that* scandalous film and the producers asked me to do a second one. **La Vampire Nue** was not so delirious. But I kept one element from **Le Viol**, the mystery, like in the old serials...

Vampires burst from grandfather clocks, lovers are speared on the same stake – you are noted for your imagery not your narratives – is this fair comment?

The answer is this. The imagery in my films is certainly more important than the story itself. But the stories are done to provoke such images. In a certain way, the stories are "mad love" stories and the images are surrealist visions. The mixture of both makes my films.

In some ways your films break gender stereotypes – often two females are the lead players – is this a conscious attempt at "sexual equality" or a male reaction in showing seductive figures, often engaged in lesbian activities, or something else?!!

Why the girls? I really don't know. Maybe a psycho-analyst can tell! Even in my books, *Les Demoiselles De L'Etrange* there are two, *The Vampire Orphans* of course and many more. About the love scenes, I must confess that, for me, I prefer to see (and show) two girls naked rather than a girl and a man. For me, a naked girl is more interesting, for sensuality and for poetry (a naked girl is *always* poetry), to put her in a clock or in a chimney, or anywhere except a bed. Using things for unexpected uses is the base of all surrealist painting. See Max Ernst, Marcel Duchamp. When Duchamp painted *Nude Walking Down A Stair*, it's no more a simple stair. It became *the* stair with a nude on it. Understand? My clock is no more a simple clock, it's a clock with the vampire girl in it [**Le Frisson**], then the girl killer hides in it [**Killing Car**]. It's become Rollin's clock!!

Regained memory and lost innocence also appear to be central themes in your work – why?

Every man is, consciously or not, researching, remembering his childhood. When I was a child, there was no TV, only movies. I saw so many films... with the innocent eyes of a child. Maybe I am trying to recapture these moments and make films with the same eyes I had to see **Mysterious Docteur Satan** or **Jungle Jim**...

These childhood memories would include such recurring locations as Dieppe beach?

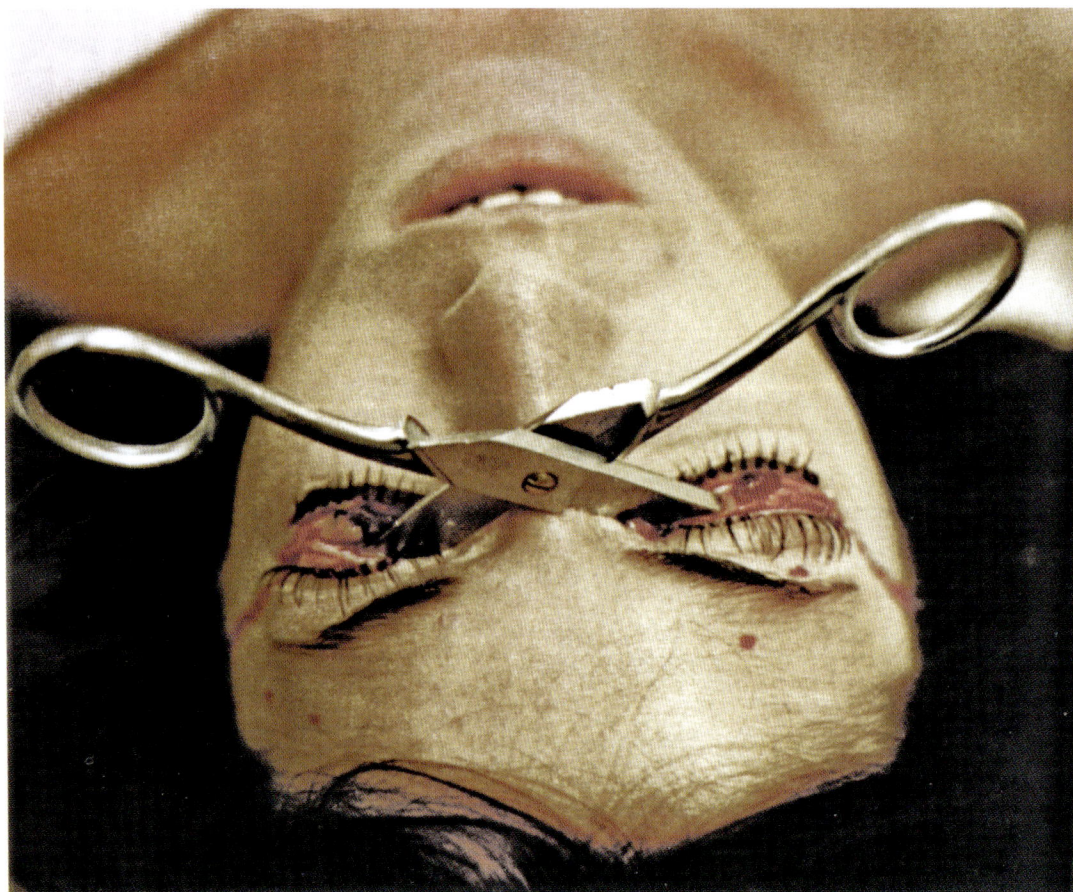

As I said I was fascinated by that strange beach. I have seen many beautiful beaches in my life, but this one, I don't know why, for me represents mystery itself. It's a surrealistic beach. Three elements: the *falaise* [cliffs], the sea and the *mouettes* [seagulls].

How have you enjoyed working with such actresses as Brigitte Lahie, Marina Pierro and Françoise Pascal?

Brigitte is a pleasure to work with. She is quiet, she really likes to act, to play, and she does what is required of her role. When I took her for **Nuit Des Traquées** I was sure she would be great in the scene where she becomes insane slowly. And that sequence was the most important in all of the film for me. And I was right. Brigitte in that part was *émouvante*. Marina Pierro is Italian. Her temperament is fiery. It was good for such a character in the film. Françoise Pascal is very professional. Working with her was interesting because, to the contrary of most girls I'd directed before, she really was into the story, trying to bring ideas, to discuss what I had in mind. Her performance in the film is great. If she can find such roles to play she can go far, but what became of her?

Lèvres De Sang *is widely regarded as your best film – which is your own favourite and why?*

I have no favourite. Maybe the next one! **Lèvres De Sang** is certainly my best script. The story was really good, based on the childhood memories that the hero had forgotten. Every person is sensitive to such a story. Everybody has had a childhood love at some time, and in the film the childhood love came true! Of course I like **Le Viol** because it was so attacked! But I also have a certain love for **Requiem** and for **Bangkok**. But the best one is **The Little Orphan Vampires**, probably.

La Rose De Fer has been described as a horror version of Romeo And Juliet – do you agree with this description?

One day, a stupid journalist, who understood nothing of my films in general and **La Rose** in particular asked me: "But at the end, what is that film about? What did it mean?" and I answered: "What! You don't see it's my version of *Romeo And Juliet*? You have the boy and the girl and the cemetery and the family trying to separate them! But maybe it's true as you can see the film like that – but for me it was just a joke.

La Vampire Nue is a personal favourite of mine for its dramatic use of colour, costumes and fetishistic imagery – it was also your first film in colour – how much of a difference did the use of colour make in your approach to the film?

After **Le Viol** I had to make a more classical film. So in place of the delirious images of **Le Viol** I tried to put some mystery into **La Vampire Nue**. Mystery of the strange people, the strange girl who is not really a vampire, and mystery with the locations in Paris I found. Places had great importance for me in that film. For example, I like the strange meeting in the beginning between the girl and the boy (my brother Olivier) under the pale light. Nothing special, only elements of everyday, except the girl with her strange costume, but the bizarre atmosphere is there. Why? Which? What? I don't know but the mystery is there.

LES DISTRIBUTEURS ASSOCIÉS (films modernes) présentent

La Vampire Nue

UN FILM DE JEAN ROLLIN • PRODUCTION FILMS A.B.C

EASTMANCOLOR

You have been roundly condemned by critics for your excursions into pornographic/ hardcore films – what is your response to such criticism?

I shoot X-films to have sufficient money to be able to live. I don't like the films but to make them can be amusing. I remember that period with pleasure. I liked the people I was working with, it was always one or two day shoots, very funny, a good friendly atmosphere. But no interesting films, that's all I can say.

*You worked on **Zombie Lake** – segments of which appeared in Jess Franco's **Virgin Among The Living Dead** – how did you get involved in this project?*

I technically shot **Zombie Lake** because Jess Franco, who was supposed to do it, had disappeared! The producers phoned me one Sunday when I was asleep and asked; "Can you shoot a zombie film tomorrow morning for two weeks?" and I said "Yes". I haven't seen the sequence in **Virgin** as I haven't seen that film, so I don't know if it's my sequence. But it's true I shot a sequence of zombies running after a girl for the same producer separately, and I don't know what was done with that footage, so maybe that's in **Virgin**.

*Your later living dead/zombie films such as **Grapes Of Death** and **The Living Dead Girl** are very different in their approaches the former with almost USA-style gore scenes, the latter more psychological as well as sanguinary. What were your intentions in each of these films?*

Grapes is probably my greatest commercial success. It's sold everywhere (except in England!). Because it's more like what is expected by the audience. The idea was to do a "living dead" film with the same horrors you would find in a Romero film, but with a different story. Romero's style is "claustrophobic", the people are holed-up in a house surrounded by the zombies. I try the contrary approach; people are running in a vast countryside area, and, most importantly, my zombies are in part living, with consciences, they know what they are doing but can't stop themselves. So the sequence where the actor becomes mad and cuts the head off his girlfriend, telling her at the same time that he loves her, is very dramatic! And such a dramatic construction was not possible with the unconscious zombies in Romero's film and many others.

For **The Living Dead Girl** it's also the memories that interest me. The girl came back to life and now inhabits her former château, in her own room, and finds her childhood toys and other souvenirs come back one by one. It's very emotional, very dramatic. And that for me, was the most interesting part of the film. The memories of the two little girls, the music box. And the end before one girl kills and eats the other one, she reminds her of when they were little girls. The massacre is a kind of love scene, like the killing with the axe in **Grapes**. The two sequences are from the same idea.

*How did you get involved with **Emanuelle 6** and was it an enjoyable/rewarding experience?*

In **Emanuelle 6**, I like the character of the little savage girl. I was thinking of Yoko, the girl in **Bangkok** for that, but she had disappeared at that moment. I directed a part of the film in France. It was a job with no problems. I like to shoot "erotic softcore films", it's a rest for me.

Fascination is another highly regarded film of yours – there's a startling opening contrast of upper-class costumed ladies drinking blood from wine glasses in an abattoir. What was the thinking behind this and how do you explain your own fascination with vampires?

My idea at the beginning was to give Brigitte Lahie a costume from the beginning of this century! And to make a film practically entirely in a château. The first image of the script was the girls drinking in the slaughterhouse. That was inspired by a short story called "The Glass Of Blood" by Jean Lorrain, an author of that period. The rest is my idea, from that: all the film shot in the château and just three people in most of the scenes. And Brigitte in a château dressed in 1900 costume period!

*Can you tell me about three of your films which have never been available within the UK – **Les Trottoirs De Bangkok**, **La Femme Dangereuse** and **Lost In New York**?*

I have spoken of **Bangkok** before. **Femme Dangereuse (Killing Car** is the real title) is a kind of strange thriller. There is a mysterious Asian girl, really so beautiful you should see her, killing people, nobody knows why. In a moment, she jumps from inside a clock to shoot! It's a minor film, but I like it, it's real B-movie style as in the good old times! **Lost In New York** is a one-hour film for TV. It's a kind of resumé of everything personal I've put in my other films. It's really shot in New York for the greatest part, and, of course, on the beach near Dieppe.

*Your latest film **Little Orphan Vampires** sees you reunited with one of your earlier collaborators – Lionel Wallman – how do you rate the film compared with your previous works and what are the key elements?*

Lionel Wallman is an old friend and he knows me very well. So, it's always a pleasure to collaborate with him. This latest film is a little different. For the first time, I had a little money and time to work with the actors before shooting. The construction is the real construction of a film, and not an improvisation. It was easy, because the script is based upon the book. Maybe for the first time, I think it's a real movie and not a strange patchwork of eroticism, violence, blood, horror and Rollin's obsessions like before.

With elaborate figures such as Batgirl, we seem assured of more of your trademark outré costumes and images though?

The batgirl is an idea which was not in the book. It's one of the very rare supernatural moments in the film. The film is realist.

*Your novels in this series run to five now – are there plans to produce film versions of these and have you a UK distributor for **Little Orphan Vampires** yet?*

If this film is a success, of course the idea is to make a sequel with the five books.

Little Orphan Vampires marks your return to the vampire genre after a ten year hiatus – why return to it now?

That's not exactly true. There is a vampire sequence in **Lost In New York** and the girl in **Killing Car** is a kind of vampire... but real vampires? Because of the five books. The idea was to put on screen the first one and then the others. Now I have in my mind a little vampire film totally set in the ruins of a medieval château... very low-budget but a classical vampire story with beautiful locations.

You have a regular team of actors and technicians who are your friends – how important are they to the unique style and spirit of your films?

They know me and I know them. They trust me and that is great. Without my crew it's impossible to make such low-budget films.

"Dreams and life – it's the same thing, or else it's not worth living" – quoted from Carné's Les Enfants Du Paradis. Your own philosophy too?

There are many beautiful images hidden inside the head of each human being. The idea is to take them and show them outside.

–Interview by Andy Black, 1996

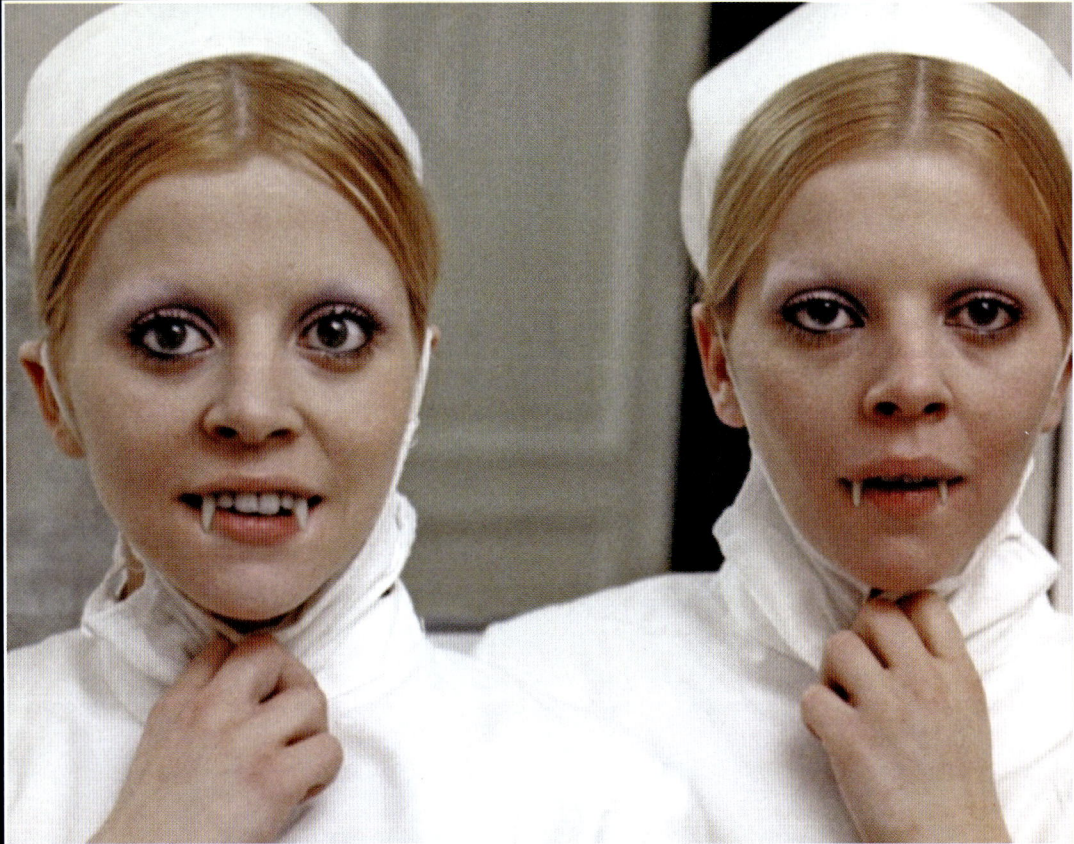

LIST OF ILLUSTRATIONS